the
FORMULA
for building great
VOLUNTEER
TEAMS

Dale Hudson

the formula for building great volunteer teams

ISBN-978-163587339-9

Library of Congress Cataloguing in Publication Data

Printed in U.S.A.

CONTENT

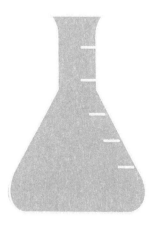

This book is dedicated to the volunteers I've had the privilege of serving with over the years. Thank you for your heart for helping others discover God's love. You've inspired me, encouraged me and challenged me to give my life to what matters most.

INTRODUCTION

Do you find it challenging to build a strong volunteer team? You're not alone. Ask any ministry leader what their biggest challenge is and you're likely to hear one word.

VOLUNTEERS

I believe the success of any ministry rises and falls on the strength of its volunteer team. If you are going to see your community reached for Christ, it is critical that you know how to build a great volunteer team.

In this book, you're going to discover a formula that can help you build that team. You'll uncover not only how to bring in new volunteers, but also how to set them up for success and see them grow and flourish long-term in their roles.

I'm excited to share the truths and principles in this book with you. It flows not out of theory alone, but out of years of hands-on experience, trial and error and proven results. It has been used to build thriving volunteer teams in all sizes of churches and it will work in your church as well.

At the end of each chapter, you'll see discussion questions. You can use these discussions to formulate practical steps that you can immediately put in motion. Whether you're brand new to this or a seasoned veteran, this book is going to help you build your team. Are you ready? Cool. Then let's dive right in and get started.

Dale

.

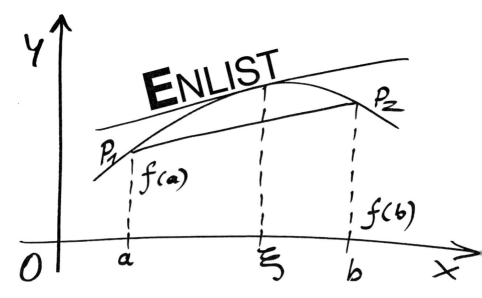

"You can design and create, and build the most wonderful place in the world. But it takes people to make the dream a reality."
Walt Disney[1]

If I had to choose one thing to excel at in ministry, it would be building volunteer teams. You can be a great communicator, great administrator, great strategist and have rock star talent, but if you don't learn how to build volunteer teams, you will be limited in what you can accomplish. A one-man show is not the way to go. Here's why.

"It's not what you can do, it's what you can empower others to do."

How important is it to build volunteer teams? Here's what I believe.

"The success of your ministry rises and falls on the strength of the volunteer team you build."

Yes! It's that important!

And if it's that important, then the $1,000,000 question is "How do you build a great volunteer team?" Is there something you can put in the coffee that will cause people to sign up to serve in the nursery? Is there a subliminal message you can place on the screens in the worship center that will spark an interest in serving on the greeter team? Better yet, maybe we can pray and ask God to send down a group of angels who will land in the choir loft, lifting their heavenly voices, causing people to fall down and cry out, "What must I do to serve?"

Probably not going to happen. It's simply not that easy. But the good news is, you can bring lots of new volunteers on your team if you'll follow the principles found in this first chapter.

The starting point, the foundation, for bringing new volunteers on your team is to…

Get the Right Perspective

What pops in your mind when you see the word **VOLUNTEER**? Take a minute and write down some of the words you're thinking about in the box below.

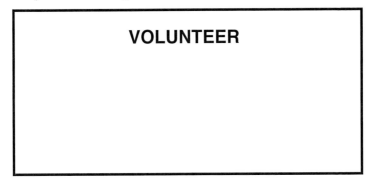

```
VOLUNTEER
```

What words did you write down? Words like unpaid? Caring? Servant? Giving? Helping? Faithful? Working for God? Okay. Keep reading. We'll come back to those words in a few minutes. First, let's look at Matthew 28:19. This verse contains our marching orders as ministry leaders.

"Therefore, go and make disciples of all the nations, baptizing them in the name of the Father and the Son and the Holy Spirit."
Matthew 28:19[2]

What does God say we are to make? Volunteers? No, **it doesn't say go and make volunteers. It says we are to go and make disciples**. Here's the right perspective to have.

"We are not called to make volunteers.
*We are called to make **disciples**."*

See the difference? When you realize this, it changes your entire perspective about bringing new volunteers onto your team. We are called to make disciples. This means we are called to come alongside people and help them grow in their faith.

And that's where serving comes in. A critical component of someone growing in their faith is serving. When we enlist someone to join our volunteer team, we are helping disciple them. We are opening a door for the person to grow in their faith.

Ephesians 4:11-16 is another passage that is written for you as a ministry leader. And it again talks about enlisting volunteers to serve. I'd like you to read this passage and circle some key words that jump out at you.

"Now these are the gifts Christ gave to the church: the apostles, the prophets, the evangelists, and the pastors and teachers. Their responsibility is to equip God's people to do His work and build up the church, the body of Christ. This will continue until we all come to such unity in our faith and knowledge of God's Son that we will be mature in the Lord, measuring up to the full and complete standard of Christ.

Then we will no longer be immature like children. We won't be tossed and blown about by every wind of new teaching. We will not be influenced when people try to trick us with lies so clever they sound like the truth. Instead, we will speak the truth in love, growing in every way more and more like Christ, who is the head of His body, the church. He makes the whole body fit together perfectly. As each part does its own special work, it helps the other parts grow, so that the whole body is healthy and growing and full of love."[3]

Okay. Now I'd like you to take the words you circled in Ephesians 4 and write them down in the right side of the chart on the next page. Then look back at page 2 and write down the words you wrote under the word volunteer on the left side of the chart.

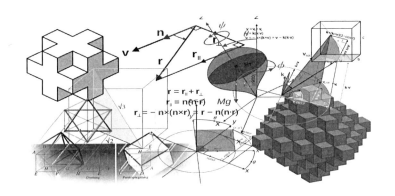

THE FORMULA FOR BUILDING GREAT VOLUNTEER TEAMS

VOLUNTEER

Words from page 2	Words you circled in Ephesians 4

As you compare the two lists, what do you notice? If you're like most people, the words you initially wrote down to describe a volunteer are words that reflect what you want **from** them. But the words you wrote down from Ephesians 4 are different, aren't they? Equip. Build up. Mature. Measuring up. Complete. Growing. Fit together. Healthy. Full of love. These describe what we want **for** people who serve.

*"Inviting people to serve shouldn't be about what you want **FROM** people, it should be about what you want **FOR** people."*

You see, serving is a critical component of being a disciple. And it's a big factor in growing in your faith. In fact, I would say that you can't be a growing disciple without serving. There is something about serving that activates a person's faith. Remember James 2? It says, *"faith without works is dead."*[4] When you see a person, whose spiritual growth is stagnated, it is often because they are not serving. Head knowledge without foot action leads to spiritual stagnation.

Think about it from that perspective. That means **when you ask someone to serve, you are giving them the opportunity to become a better disciple!**

It's about helping someone mature in their faith through leading a 3rd grade boys' small group. It's about helping someone grow to be more like Christ by holding a door and greeting people. It's about helping someone get connected with the body of Christ through relationships formed while serving.

When you shift to this perspective, it will set you free from the hesitation you may feel about asking people to serve. You'll realize that you're not bothering people when you ask them to serve. You are blessing them! You are giving them an opportunity to grow in their faith and become a better disciple. Walk in this confidence!

Time and time again, I have heard volunteers talk about how serving has helped them grow in their faith. Steve is a good friend of mine. He is a man's man. He is a weight lifter, boxer, bodybuilder and successful business leader. He also serves in children's ministry. We were preparing a vision casting video for our children's small group ministry and I asked Steve to share about serving in this area. I didn't script what he was going to say, we wanted it to come from his heart. And here's how he started his testimony.

"You know, when I first started serving in children's ministry, it was really the impact and transformation it had in my life."
Steve

Wow! What a privilege we have to present people with the opportunity to grow in their faith through serving!

When you invite someone to serve, you are also giving them an opportunity to be like Jesus.

"For even the Son of Man came not to be served but to serve others and to give His life as a ransom for many."
Mark 10:45[5]

Jesus' life could be summed up in the two words you find in that verse. **Serve and Give.** We are never more like Jesus than when we are serving others. I love the following quote.

"Everyone can be great, because everyone can serve."
Dr. M.L. King[6]

What a great way to help a believer grow their faith by inviting them to serve like Jesus!

It's also important to understand that **everyone is called to serve**. Look what Ephesians 2:10 says.

"For we are God's handiwork, created in Christ Jesus to do good works, which God prepared in advance for us to do."
Ephesians 2:10[7]

We've often heard the 80/20 rule. 20% of the people in the church do 80% of the work. Should it be that way? Not according to the verse above. Were only 20% of believers created to serve? No! 100% of believers were created to serve!

Invite to the WHY over the WHAT

Grab hold of this one principle and it will be a game changer for your ministry! Did you know **HOW** you invite people to join your team makes all the difference? Inviting people to the "why" instead of the "what" is a small tweak that will pay huge dividends. The "what" is the tasks of the role, while the "why" is the reason behind the tasks. Plain and simple...the "what" is what you do...the "why" is why you do what you do.

Our natural tendency is to invite people to the tasks of the what. We ask people to hold babies in the nursery. We ask people to lead a small group for students. We ask people to teach an adult Bible study. We ask people to help park cars. We ask people to help preschoolers put together their crafts. But this is not the most effective way to build a team. Why? We are inviting people to the what. **And people are not drawn to tasks, they are drawn to a cause that is bigger than themselves! People want to know that their life matters for something. Instead of inviting people to the what, invite people to the why.**

I often say this…

> *"People won't line up to change a diaper,*
> *but they will line up to change a life."*

When you reverse the ask and present the why first, you will begin to see new volunteers join your team. Here are a few practical examples.

You are looking for someone to serve in the nursery. Here's a "what" ask:

"We need someone to serve in the nursery during the 10:00 a.m. service. You would be receiving the babies from the parents, rocking the babies, changing their diapers and reading a Bible story to them. Are you interested?"

Instead of focusing on the "what," this time let's ask someone to join our team by focusing on the "why." Here's a "why" ask:

"Did you know research confirms that the first three years are the most critical in shaping a child's brain? Early experiences provide the base for the brain's organizational development and functioning throughout life.[8]

In our nursery ministry, we know this and we serve to give the children a spiritual foundation. We also realize that in the race to a child's heart, the first one there wins[9] *and we want to get there first with Jesus' love.*

And we know this weekend, a young couple will walk through the doors for the very first time. They haven't been involved in church and they don't know Jesus, but they recently had a baby and it's been a wake-up call for them. They've decided to give this 'church thing' one opportunity. And so, they will come to the nursery. And because you are there to welcome them and their baby, they will feel comfortable leaving him or her with you in the nursery. They'll go to the worship service, where they will hear the Gospel for the first time and the projection of their family will be changed forever! How would you like to be part of impacting families for eternity by serving with us?"

See the difference?

Here's another example. Let's say you are looking for someone to join your greeter team. Here's a "what" ask."

"I'm looking for someone to join our greeter team. You would be welcoming people and helping new families register. Are you interested in serving as a greeter?"

Now let's make the ask by focusing on the "why" instead of the "what."

"Our guests decide in the first 8 minutes if they're going to return to our church. People who serve as greeters are a vital part of this. When they help people feel welcome, show people where to go and help people check-in, it makes a huge difference and opens people's hearts to be receptive to the Gospel later in the service. How would you like to be the person that God uses to make that kind of difference in people's lives?"

Notice again the difference?

Let's look at one more example. You need someone to lead a 4th grade boys' small group. Here's a "what" ask:

"We need someone to lead a 4th grade boys' small group. You would be leading the kids in activities and discussions about the lesson and praying with them. Would you like to do this?"

Now let's approach it with a "why" ask.

"Kids' lives aren't changed because of cool music or amazing rooms or the latest technology. It's small group leaders that God uses to make the impact. When a child knows someone cares about them and takes a personal interest in them, it makes all the difference in the world. When you serve as a small group leader, you help kids grow in their faith and become lifelong followers of Jesus. How would you like to leave that kind of legacy?"

You obviously have to share with people the what...but it should be in the shadow of the why.

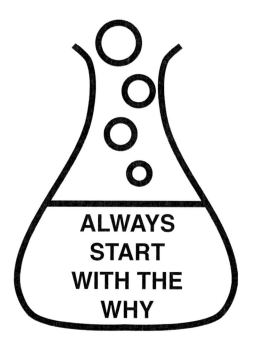

ALWAYS START WITH THE WHY

One-On-One Personal Invites

Why do people volunteer? Here are the top 10 reasons from bottom to top.

10. **External Forces**
    (saw an ad in the bulletin, heard an announcement)

9. **Boredom**
    (didn't have anything else to do, looking for something to fill their time)

8. **Guilt**
    (example – were told "if you don't serve, the kids won't be able to have class today" or" if you don't serve, the homeless won't get a meal today")

7. **Need Experience**
    (example – someone who is going to be a school teacher and wants experience working with kids)

6. **Social Need**
    (they want to be part of something that connects them to a social group)

5. **Spiritual Reasons**
    (they believe it will help them get closer to God)

4. **Gratitude**
    (they want to give back because of the blessings they have received)

3. **Personal Connection** (example – someone who volunteers in a cancer awareness event because they have a family member with cancer)

2.   **Compelling need**
       (a big issue they see as important or an event that they
       want to see succeed)

1.   **Personal Invitation**
       (someone personally invites them to serve with them)

Notice the number one reason people volunteer. Someone personally asked them. In fact, stats show that this is consistently why 87-93% of people volunteer. Stop for a second and think about it. Are you serving because someone personally asked you to? Probably so. That's me. When I was sixteen years old, I was your typical teenage boy. All I cared about was sports, my car and girls. But then my youth pastor approached me about serving in children's ministry. At first, I said "no," but he didn't give up. He continued to ask me and finally I said "yes." Once I started serving, God grabbed my heart and changed my life. At the time of this writing, I have now been serving in children's ministry for over 33 years. And it all started by someone personally asking me.

One person at a time. That's how Jesus built His team. Look what Matthew says.

"As Jesus went on from there, He saw a man named Matthew sitting at the tax collector's booth. 'Follow Me,' He told him, and Matthew got up and followed Him."
Matthew 9:9[10]

Jesus approached people one at a time and invited them to follow Him. I believe it is the most effective way to build a team. When it comes to personally asking people to serve, I believe there is a big factor that makes the difference. It is often the difference between someone saying "yes" or "no." What is it?

DIVINE APPOINTMENTS

Before you make the ask, pray and ask God to lead you to the people He is dealing with about serving. Ask Him to give you a divine appointment. A great example of a divine appointment is found in the story of Phillip and the Ethiopian eunuch in Acts 8. Phillip is busy in Samaria with a thriving ministry with lots of people, when God tells him to leave and go to the Judean wilderness where He has one man waiting for him. Phillip obeys and when he gets there, he meets this man whose heart God had already prepared. The eunuch is ready to commit his life to Christ. It was a divine appointment.

I believe, just like God set up a divine appointment for Phillip, He will set up divine appointments for you. There are people in your church or ministry that God is already preparing to serve. And when You ask Him, He will lead you to those people.

Dan had been attending our church for over a year, but was not serving anywhere. We noticed him as he dropped off his kids each week. One weekend, before people started arriving, we prayed for a divine appointment for a serving opportunity we had available. Later, as we saw Dan checking in his kids, we sensed he was the one God was preparing for this role. We approached him and shared the service opportunity that was available. He immediately teared up and told us God had been dealing with him about serving in the very role we were talking to him about. He had prayed to God to send someone to ask him to serve if this was His will. We were the answer to his prayer and of course he said "yes." That's what we need when we ask people to serve. Divine appointments. Ask God and He'll arrange them for you.

You've heard the statement "The journey of a thousand miles begins with one step?" Here's what I believe.

"The journey of _____ volunteers begins with one ask."

How many volunteers do you need? 5? 50? 500? Write the number you need in the blank. How are you going to get there? One ask at a time. One new volunteer at a time.

A great way to keep this in front of you and your team is to create a visual reminder. If you were to walk down the office area of the children's ministry I led, you would see posters on the walls. Each poster was labeled with a ministry area such as nursery, preschool, elementary, pre-teens, greeters, etc. And on each poster, there were sticky notes. Each sticky note represented a volunteer position that we needed to fill. It was a constant reminder to pray and make personal asks. As we filled the roles, we marked out the sticky notes.

In the children's ministry I led, we started with 300 volunteers. Eight years later, there were over 2,600 volunteers. How did it happen? One new volunteer at a time. We didn't sit down and say, "Let's build a volunteer team of 2,600." We simply approached one person and asked them to serve. And the next week we approached another person. Week in and week out, month after month, year after year, we personally asked people to join the team. And one day, we looked up and we had 2,600 of those "one" volunteers.

If you want to build a great volunteer team, then you must be committed to inviting people one at a time to serve. Hold yourself accountable for doing this. Hold your staff accountable for doing this. Hold your current volunteers accountable for doing this. Constantly ask, "who did you invite to serve this week?" Lead by example by constantly inviting people to serve. Set a goal for everyone to ask at least one new person to serve every single week. And don't fall into the trap of depending on stage announcements, ministry fairs, bulletin ads or big pushes once a year. Nothing can take the place of personal, one-on-one asks. There is no quick, easy way to build a great volunteer team. It's about consistently, faithfully asking people. Week in and week out. 52 weeks a year.

Duck in the Water

Have you ever noticed how a duck glides across the water, ever so gracefully?

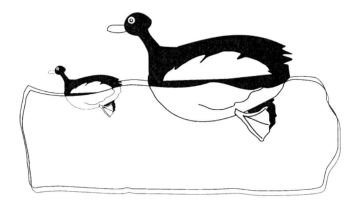

On the surface, it is calm, cool and collected. Even though the duck is paddling furiously just below the surface, you would never know it. That's the way you must portray yourself and the ministry if you want to build a great volunteer team. You may be desperate for volunteers, but don't show it. Don't let them see you sweat. Here's why.

"People are drawn to vision not desperation."

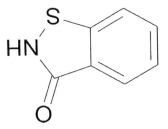

Simply put…no one wants to get on the Titanic. When you are desperate, people will look at the ministry as a sinking ship and avoid it. Here are some indicators that you're asking people to get on board the Titanic.

- You place ads in the bulletin that use words like "help" or "need" or "please."

- You try to guilt people into serving.

- The only time you connect with parents is when you are asking them to serve.

- You make it mandatory to serve if you have a child in the nursery.

- You ask the pastor to beg for volunteers for you during the service.

- You broadcast that you won't be able to open some classrooms if some people don't step up to serve.

- People equate having to serve in your ministry with "doing time."

- People abandon ship the first chance they get and warn their friends not to board.

But what people do want to get on board is a Carnival cruise ship. Instead of desperation, there is delight. Here are some signs your ministry is a Carnival cruiseship.

- It's full of happy people who are smiling and laughing.

- People are getting on board because they heard about what a great experience it is.

- People are getting on board because a friend invited them.

- People are refreshed and energized by the journey.

- There is a clear destination and people want to go there.

- It's fun.

- New friendships are formed and existing friendships are deepened.

- Great snacks and food is provided for passengers.

- The staff is there to support passengers and meet their needs.

So how are you portraying the ministry you lead? Titanic or Carnival cruise ship? Yes, I know. There are times you are desperate for volunteers and the temptation will be to resort to begging for people. Don't do it! It will have the opposite effect.

I found this out the hard way. Years ago, it was two weeks before VBS and I still needed 20 teachers to make it happen. Desperate, I told the pastor about the situation and asked if he would make an appeal for volunteers at the end of the service. He graciously agreed to do so. At the end of the service, he told the congregation what the need was and made an appeal for people to step up and teach. He told them when we dismissed, that I would be up front and they could connect with me if they wanted to help. I was so excited! I just knew the altars would flood with people coming to me, saying "What must I do to serve in VBS?" I had my clipboard ready to record the long list of names I was about to get. The final prayer was said. I excitedly went to the front and…no one came. No one. In fact, people avoided eye contact with me and ran the other way. I learned that day that people are drawn to vision not to desperation. I also learned that if I want 20 new people to volunteer for VBS, then my team and I should personally ask them.

Often I am asked how to attract high capacity volunteers. The answer is to present a great vision rather than a great need. Recently, I was talking with a high capacity volunteer in our ministry. He owns a successful financial business. In addition, he has his own radio program and is often interviewed on live television for Fox, CNN and MSNBC business reports.

I asked him what attracted him to our ministry? He said he wanted to maximize the resources and influence God has placed in his hands and a big vision could help him do that. And he said he wanted to be part of a vision that would grow and stretch him as a leader. How big is your vision? Is it big enough to attract volunteers who want to make a big-time impact? Increase your vision and you will increase the capacity of your volunteers. High capacity leaders want to be part of something bigger than themselves. This means if a vision is not going to challenge them, they will be reluctant to engage with it.

"The secret to attracting high capacity leaders is having a high capacity vision."

1 Time = Full Time

As mentioned, I don't believe stage announcements or big pushes can take the place of personal asks. But there are a few times each year when it can be very effective. Let's talk about that. There are times when your church collectively needs a lot of extra volunteers. These are events like Easter services, Fall Festival, preparing Thanksgiving meals for the community, Christmas services, etc. These are great times for the pastor and church leadership to encourage people to sign up to serve one time. The ask can be done during the main worship service from the stage. **Have a response mechanism ready, whether it's a card they fill out and turn in or a text message or other form of digital registration.** You want people to respond and sign-up on the spot. Have all the big areas of serving opportunities listed such as parking lot, greeters, children's ministry, hospitality, etc.

An example would be Christmas services. Since you are having extra services, you can ask people, who don't normally serve, to sign up to serve in the parking lot, as greeters, as hosts and other easier roles. If you do this church-wide, you will have a solid number of people sign up. As previously stated, **make the ask with the "why" more than the "what."** Let the congregation know there are a lot of families coming who don't normally attend church and it's a great opportunity to impact them and introduce them to the love of Jesus. Help them see that's "why" you are asking for extra volunteers.

Now going into this, **your strategy and goal is to help people have a great experience during their one-time serve.** Some things you can do to help this happen are **provide them with snacks/drinks, give them clear instructions and give them an easy, non-leadership role.** Don't expect a one-time serve person that you shove in a room with 30 three-year-olds and one teenager to have a good experience.

Why is this so important? Because after their one-time serve, you're going to come back to them and ask if they'd like to join the team on a regular basis. Another great tip is to **place your one-time serve people with your "rock star" volunteers.** By rock star volunteers, I mean your best volunteers. You know, the volunteers who are positive, faithful and fun to be around. The volunteers who love serving and whose joy is contagious. You want that to rub off on your one-time serve volunteers!

The next step is where this pays off. **After the event is over, connect back with the one-time serve people and invite them to join your team on a full-time basis.** I have found that if you are intentional about this, you will get a high percentage of them to come on board long-term. I have seen as many as 75-80% of the one-time volunteers become full-time volunteers when we asked them. It's also important to **make the follow-up ask the very next week after they serve.**

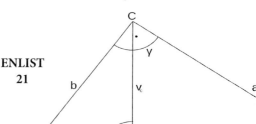

Charles and his wife, Jessica, are a great example of this. They signed up to serve as one-time volunteers at one of our Fall Festivals. We did our best to make sure they had a great serving experience at the event and a few days after I called them and asked if they would be interested in serving on a regular basis with us. They said "yes." Long story short, they are now both staff members who are making a huge impact on the ministry. And it's because we were intentional about turning a one-time serve into a full-time serve. It will work for you as well.

KNOW WHERE TO GO

When I'm traveling, I'm always looking for Wi-Fi hot spots. Whether it's in an airport, restaurant, coffee shop or hotel, I'm looking for a place where I can get connected. I know if I find a hot spot, I can get work done. Let me ask you, **do you know where the volunteer hot spots are in your church or ministry**? By this, I mean the places that are good spots to connect with potential volunteers.

Our church had a guest reception after the service. We invited first-time guests or people who had been visiting for awhile, but hadn't gotten connected, to come there so we could meet them and tell them more about the church. Guess where I liked to hang out after the service? At the guest reception. I knew it was a potential volunteer hot spot. At one of these guest receptions, I noticed a lady who had a bright smile and bubbly personality. I sat down at the table and introduced myself. Her name was Tracy and she had just moved from Hawaii where she had finished graduate school. As we talked, I found out that she had been a children's ministry volunteer in the past. After the reception, I took her on a tour of our children's area and introduced her to some of our volunteers. I invited her to join our volunteer team and she said "yes." Fast forward five years later. Tracy is now the children's ministry director at one of the church's largest campuses, where she leads hundreds of volunteers and kids. All of this happened, because we went to a potential volunteer "hot spot."

Find out where the potential volunteer hot spots are in your church and spend time there. It might be a guest reception, a new member's class, a men's event, a women's event, a student ministry gathering, a Bible study or a small group. One thing is for sure, **the hot spots are somewhere outside of your ministry.** To get there, you'll need to empower others to do the work of the ministry you lead so you can get to those hot spots and make connections.

EVERY MEMBER SERVES

Speaking of hot spots, let's talk about a strategy that can help you have a steady stream of new volunteers coming in. Outside of personal asks, I believe it is one of the top strategies to build a volunteer team. Here it is – **set the standard that every member serves.** Create a culture that says a big part of joining our church family, is committing to serve. That's what family does. Everyone chips in and does their part.

The most effective way to do this is through your new member's class. In the next to last class, teach about the value of serving and impacting others. Give everyone a list of the serving opportunities in the church and ask them to prayerfully think about where they would like to serve. Then, in the last class, have a representative from each ministry present. Have new members decide where they would like to serve and connect them right then and there with the leader of that ministry area. Having them take the step right then, helps eliminate people falling through the cracks and never being placed in a serving role.

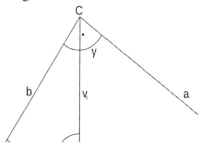

One of the fastest growing churches in the country does this so well. In the last class, they have the ministry leaders take the new members and do initial volunteer training right then. It's no wonder they are retaining a very high percentage of their guests. The reason?

"Serving is the super glue that keeps people connected and active in a church."

Attendance used to drive engagement at church. Families attended consistently…only missing 2-3 weekends a year. But this has shifted. Families are still attending church, but less frequently. As I talk with ministry leaders across the country and from my own personal experience of leading a local church ministry, I have found that the average family with children only attends church once every three to four weeks. And for many, it's even less than that.

But there is a group that is consistently there on a weekly basis. Who are they? People who are serving! When people are serving, they develop relationships with the people they serve with. When people are serving, they know someone is counting on them to be there. When people are serving, they have bought into the vision of the church. When people are serving, they are connected. In today's culture, I believe the best way to grow a church is by engaging people in serving. If you want to grow, you must develop a culture that encourages every member to serve.

STUDENTS

There is a mighty army of volunteers in your church, just waiting for you ask them to serve. They are full of life, energy and passion. When they are on fire for God, they can breathe new life into a tired ministry. In many cases, they have extra time on their hands and are looking for ways to invest it. Who are they? Students (or teenagers if you want to call them by that name).

Some of the best volunteers I have served with were students. I've seen God use them to make a huge impact. Especially in the lives of kids. Kids look up to students and want to be like them. What a unique opportunity students have to make an impact for God's kingdom when you empower them and release them to do ministry.

Recently I saw where the Teen Choice Awards honored some students who are making a difference. Check out three of them.

Chad Bullock: This student from North Carolina is leading a fight against tobacco. After losing family members to lung cancer, Chad got involved in anti-tobacco activism. He works in politics and convinced the attorney general to take action against tobacco ads aimed at kids, He was even able to turn the Durham Bulls Arena into a smoke-free facility.[11]

Kathryn Cunningham: This teenage girl volunteered at a hospital in Gambia where she helped perform an emergency medical procedure by candlelight. Kathryn has been active in helping the people in Gambia after seeing a newborn die due to the lack of electricity. She started a company called Power Up Gambia, that provides solar panels to the country.[12]

Dallas Jessup: This Tae Kwon Do black belt may only be a student, but she is powerful. After multiple attacks in her neighborhood, at 16 years of age, she taught students how to defend themselves by creating a video. Her video has been distributed 750,000 times.[13]

Pat Pedraja: Pat was diagnosed with leukemia at the age of 10. Being in a minority, there were no donors in the National Marrow Donor Program Registry that matched him. He watched many other people die due to the lack of donors. At age 13, Pat drove cross-country (32 cities) with his mom to raise awareness of this problem. He raised $140,000 and added 7,000 donors.[14]

These are just a few examples of what students can do when you give them an opportunity to serve. So how can you get the students in your church involved in serving?

First, begin building a relationship with student ministry staff and volunteers. Share with them the vision of helping students grow as disciples through serving. (remember - it's not what you want from them, it's what you want for them).

Next, go to them. We just talked about hot spots. Go to the student ministry hot spots in your church. This may be leading a student small group, helping at an event, leading a Bible study, driving the van, etc.

Be yourself. Students want authentic relationships. Don't try to be cool. They'll see right through it. Unless you are 21 and under, they are looking at you like you're ancient anyways. Just be yourself.

Share the vision. Students are just like everyone else. They are drawn to vision. They want to be part of something that's bigger than themselves. Show them the opportunity they have to make a big impact for God's Kingdom.

Challenge students who are currently serving to share the vision of serving with their peers. Students usually come to serve in groups. A great way to do this is to invite a student ministry small group to serve together. I've even seen small groups who meet for their Bible study and prayer time and go from that right into their time of serving.

Make sure they stay connected to student ministry. Sometimes you will have push back from student ministry leadership when you ask about students serving. Normally this is because they are worried about the students getting disconnected from student ministry. And this can happen. I have seen students who didn't quite fit into student ministry use children's ministry as a place to hide or I have seen them start skipping the student ministry program. It is vital to help students see the importance of staying connected to student ministry if they are serving in other areas. This helps them stay healthy spiritually, connected relationally and serving from the overflow of what is being poured into them. Which leads me to the next important step.

Set clear expectations, structures and guidelines for serving. All volunteers need this, but especially students due to their maturity level. Set these up front by meeting with them and going over them. Have it in writing and have them sign an agreement to abide by it. The purpose is to call them up to be all that God wants them to be. Again, when they know you really care about them and want to invest in them, they will respond with an open heart.

Involve their parents. When you meet with anyone under 18 who would like to serve, it is important that their parents be present at the meeting as well. Make sure their parents are on board with the time commitment and responsibilities their student is committing to. This will also help you later if you need to hold the student accountable for their behavior. Have the parent sign the agreement listed above as a witness for their child.

A few years ago, our church began taking a hard look at how we did summer camp. We realized that taking students off to a camp, where it was all about them, was not producing the spiritual growth we wanted to see. There had to be something more impactful than floating down a lazy river or riding on a horse or playing volleyball. So, we decided to try something radical. Rather than going off to camp, we decided that we'd take the week and offer students the opportunity to serve in a poor community. During the day, they would plant trees, paint houses, clean parks, paint local schools and help with a host of other community service projects...in the hot South Florida sun...8 hours a day…for 5 days. At night, they would have a time of worship and a message and then sleep on air mattresses in the classrooms of a local public school.

What happened? The response was overwhelming. More kids signed up to be a part of it than would have signed up for a camp. We've been doing this for several years now and it has grown every year. Now it sells out the first day registration opens and there is a waiting list. Students' lives have been changed and many have been called into ministry. Students want to give their lives to something that matters. They're just waiting for you to believe in them. They're just waiting for you to call them up to all God is ready to do in them and through them. Will you enlist them?

KIDS AND PARENTS SERVING TOGETHER

Another great opportunity you have to involve people in serving is inviting kids and parents to serve together. Here are a few examples.

- Invite kids and parents to serve together as greeters.

- Invite kids and parents to serve on community service projects. The 4th Saturday morning of each month we provided service projects families could do together. This included things like painting a widow's house, re-doing the flower beds at a local public school, cleaning up a local park, etc.

- Invite kids and parents to put together meals and care packages for those in need. Each year at Thanksgiving, we gave kids and parents the opportunity to assemble meals together and deliver them to families in need. And a few times each year, we dismissed the morning service early and had stations set up where families could assemble meals that would be delivered to those in need in other countries.

- Invite kids and parents to pass out bulletins together.

- Kids and parents can serve in the church café together.

Remember what we talked about earlier. If you want to see families be more consistent in their attendance, then engage them in serving. Families that are serving will be faithful. It is also great for kids to see their parents modeling what it means to serve.

KIDS

People will often say, "Kids are the church of tomorrow." That is true. But they are also the church of today. They don't have to wait until they are adults to start serving and making a difference. In fact, the reason many adults are sitting on the pew and not serving is because when they were kids, we told them to "sit still and be quiet." They're just doing what we told them to do! It's time we invite kids to serve now and help them discover the gifts and talents God has placed in them. There are many ways kids can serve. They can help greet, help collect the offering, help clean up, sing on the praise team, pass out bulletins, be on the prayer team, help run the audio/video and much more. If we allow kids to start serving at a young age, they will grow up knowing it's what Christ-followers do.

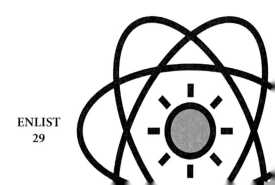

MILLENNIALS

Much is being written about the Millennials. Born between 1981 and 1997, they are age 20 to 36 at the time of this writing.[15] They have unique characteristics you need to know if you want to see them join your volunteer team. Here is some insight that will help you make the ask.

Millennials want a purpose to serve for. 87% of Millennials believe the success of an organization should be measured by its purpose.[16] They want to serve in organizations that have a cause. This syncs with what we talked about earlier. Inviting to the why more than to the what. This especially applies to Millennials. They are far more interested in a purpose than they are a position.

Millennials will give their life to something if they believe in it. When they find something worth committing to, they will be jump in and give their very best to it. We will talk more about how to equip and keep Millennials later in this book.

SENIOR ADULTS

We hear a lot about "next gen" ministry and I'm all for it. I've given my life to reaching the next generation. But a healthy family is made up of all generations. How about "all gen" ministry? I believe a healthy volunteer team is made up of all generations…including senior adults. In fact, if you're overlooking senior adults as potential volunteers, you're missing out on so much potential. Let's take a look.

The Silent Generation was born between 1925 and 1945. They are ages 72 to 92 at the time of this writing. They were born during the Great Depression and World War II and were labeled the Silent Generation in 1951 by Time magazine. Their "silent" label refers to their conformist and civic instincts. Some well-known people of the Silent Generation are Dr. Martin Luther King, Clint Eastwood, Marilyn Monroe, Margaret Thatcher and Elvis Presley.[17]

Baby Boomers are the younger side of senior adults. They were born between 1946 – 1964. They are ages 53 to 71 at the time of this writing. They are called Baby Boomers because they were part of the post World War II baby boom. They grew up in the 1960's and 70's. Some well-known Boomers are Donald Trump, Denzel Washington, Oprah Winfrey, Bill Gates and Katie Couric.[18]

You may be thinking senior adults have the "I've done my time and now I'm resting" attitude. Not these senior adults! Look what David Eisner, CEO of the Corporation for National and Community service says.

"The Boomer wave signals one of the largest opportunities the nonprofit sector has ever had to expand its pool of resources. America's Baby Boomers are an untapped resource of extraordinary proportions. They are the largest, healthiest, best-educated generation in history – and they can leave an incredible legacy through service to others. Only the nonprofits that retool their ability to engage citizens will reap that reward."[19]

And look what Robert Grimm, Director of the Corporation's Office of Research and Development says.

"The baby boomer generation gives our nation an unprecedented opportunity to increase the breadth and the scope of volunteering. If we use the right approach, this population will continue their service and change the face of volunteering in America."[20]

Senior adults, especially the Boomers, are a great group to invite to join your team. As you invite them, here are some helpful tips and things to keep in mind.

Look for Boomers who are only working part-time. Almost half of Boomers who work part-time also volunteer.

Appeal to Boomer men. 29.4% of them volunteer which is higher than any other age group of men.[21]

The biggest single inducement for Boomers to volunteer is being asked by someone with whom he/she has an established relationship. They are more attracted to social interaction than to duty or obligation. Go to where they are and build relationships with them. This may look like being involved in the women's and men's ministry in your church, leading an adult Bible study, helping with senior adult activities or just spending time with them after the service in the lobby.

Boomers are achievement-oriented, dedicated, and career-focused. They welcome exciting, challenging projects and strive to make a difference. Cast vision and challenge them to step up and have a part in making a vision become a reality. They will respond.

Boomers want higher-skill assignments to keep them engaged. Provide them with professional development opportunities. Give them opportunities to be promoted in their leadership responsibilities as well.

Ask for a minimum of a three-month commitment. Stats show if they serve for at least three months, they are most likely to continue serving year after year. In fact, when they serve for at least three months, the retention rate goes up to 79 percent.[22]

Some of the greatest volunteers I've served with were senior adults. Mr. Will, as we affectionately call him, is in his 80's. He walked into our church as an unbeliever. In fact, after the first service, he approached the pastor and said, "I don't believe any of that stuff you just talked about." But he felt loved and kept coming back. It wasn't long until He stepped across the line of faith and became a follower of Jesus. God changed His life. He jumped into serving wholeheartedly. He volunteers 40-50 hours a week helping at the church. He's there more than some of the paid staff. In addition to this, he serves on weekends and makes a huge impact. Go Silent Generation!

Another one of my heroes in ministry was a lady named Dorothy who taught in a ministry I led. She was in her 80's and had been teaching for decades. As she began to grow feebler, I asked if she wanted to retire. Her class was on the second floor and I knew it was getting difficult for her to get up there. She quickly reminded me that there was an elevator and she would keep on teaching. She was stubborn that way...a good kind of stubborn. I was able to talk her into letting me get a younger leader to assist her. Dorothy taught faithfully until she passed away. I conducted her funeral. I know she heard the words "well done good and faithful servant" when she entered heaven. Her faithfulness still inspires me.

And then there's Betty. I'll never forget the first time I met her. I was a young pastor in my first full-time ministry role. I was helping a friend from college start a church in California. God had blessed our efforts and hundreds of people were attending. This was back in the day when many churches used buses to bring kids to church. One of my responsibilities was overseeing this part of the children's ministry.

One day, I was working in the church office, when through the window, I saw a big, old Cadillac pull into the parking lot. You know...one of those that's like a mile long. A little old lady got out of the car. She must have been in her 80's. And it was obvious she was wearing a wig. She began to stare inquisitively at the back of the parking lot. I went outside and introduced myself. She pointed to the back of the parking lot where we kept the buses that we used to pick up kids and asked me, "Are those buses?" I replied, "Yes they are." Betty then asked me if we used the buses to bring kids to church. I told her, "yes." She got a twinkle in her eye and said, "Years ago, the church I attend brought kids to church on buses. I volunteered and loved helping bring them to church. My church doesn't do this anymore. I sure miss those days." I thanked her for stopping by and she left.

A few weeks later, on a Sunday morning, guess who pulled into the parking lot? Yes...Betty in that big old Cadillac. She attended the service that morning and started coming faithfully. A few months after she started attending, she approached me after the service and told me she wanted to start volunteering on the children's ministry bus. I asked if she was sure she was up to it. I reminded her that it gets hot in the summer in Southern California and there was no air conditioning on the bus. She said she wanted to do it and I wasn't going to stop her (she was stubborn like Dorothy).

And so, Betty, in her 80's, began volunteering on the bus that brought kids to church. I'd watch the bus come in and there she would be...sitting in a seat surrounded by little girls that she was caring for and telling about Jesus...the sweat dripping from under her wig and down her forehead. Betty had such a passion to see kids come to Christ and she was burdened for the thousands of other kids in the city that we hadn't been able to reach yet. She asked if we had another bus, could we bring more kids to church to hear about Jesus? I told her "yes, we could." Not long after, one weekday, I saw the old Cadillac pull into the church parking lot again. I went out to greet Betty. She brought me to the back of the car and opened the trunk. Inside was an amazing collection of antique dolls... still in the original boxes. She explained that she had been collecting them for many years and they were worth a good sum of money. She told me she was going to sell them and use the money to buy another bus so we could bring more kids to hear about Jesus. I was blown away. I asked if she was sure. I knew the collection must mean a lot to her. It would be a big sacrifice on her part. Betty said her husband had told her she couldn't sell the dolls, but she said, "He doesn't tell me what to do." (I told you she was stubborn like that.) And so, she took the dolls and sold them and we used the money to purchase another bus to bring more kids to church to hear about Jesus.

Betty taught me what really matters in life. She taught me that there's no "retiring" from volunteering. She taught me that you should keep serving and making a difference as long as God has you here. Betty taught me to never stop striving to reach more kids and families for Jesus...no matter the cost or sacrifice. Betty taught me to serve even when it's not convenient or easy.

God's not done with the senior adults in your church. He still has great things He wants to do in them and through them. They have much to offer. They're just waiting for you to ask them.

VOLUNTEER MULTIPLICATION

We've talked about the power of personally asking people to join the team. But, you as the leader, can only ask so many people by yourself.

When you are personally enlisting people for the team, it is volunteer addition. But if you want to see your team explode with new volunteers, then you must have volunteer multiplication.Volunteer multiplication happens

when not only you are bringing new volunteers on the team, but your volunteers are bringing new volunteers on the team as well. Take a look at this.

1 person bringing a new volunteer each month =
12 new volunteers in one year.

2 people each bringing a new volunteer each month =
24 new volunteers in one year.

3 people each bringing a new volunteer each month =
36 new volunteers in one year.

No matter how good you are personally at enlisting volunteers, the ministry will benefit more from others adding volunteers at the same time. A great example of this is found in John 1. Check it out.

"Andrew, Simon Peter's brother, was one of these men who heard what John said and then followed Jesus. Andrew went to find his brother, Simon, and told him, 'We have found the Messiah' (which means 'Christ'). Then Andrew brought Simon to meet Jesus. Looking intently at Simon, Jesus said, 'Your name is Simon, son of John - but you will be called Cephas' (which means 'Peter')."
John 1:40-42[23]

In this passage, we see that Andrew was so excited about following Jesus that he went and found someone else to join him in the journey. When your volunteers get excited about serving in the ministry, they will bring other people to serve with them. That's volunteer multiplication.

A culture of volunteer multiplication happens when you **emphasize it** to your volunteers, **encourage** each person to bring at least one other person on the team and **honor** those who do so.

One weekend, we decided to set up a new volunteer sign-up area in our children's hallway. And instead of having staff at the booth, we asked Lisa to be there. Lisa was a volunteer who loved serving. She accepted the challenge and in one weekend she personally signed up 86 new volunteers. Yes, you read it right. She signed up 86 new volunteers in one weekend.

The truth is it holds more weight when a volunteer asks someone to serve than it does when a staff member asks. Volunteer multiplication works!

MORE OPPORTUNITIES = MORE VOLUNTEERS

Not everyone wants to start out teaching, leading worship or overseeing a program. If you'll provide lots of easy, entry-level positions, you'll find that people start out in these entry-level positions and then down the road gain enough confidence and experience to step into roles with more responsibility. If you limit your serving opportunities to just a few roles, you will limit your number of volunteers. The more serving opportunities you have, the more volunteers you will have. Here's an example. We created a safety and security team. This team helps with bathroom runs, securing doors, monitoring hallway traffic flow, filling out incident reports and more. We have some people who serve on this team that would not want to serve inside the classroom, but who love helping in this capacity. And many times, we've seen people start out on the safety and security team and later move into roles inside the classroom, as they watched and observed it from their role outside the classroom.

When you expand the number of serving opportunities, you will see the number of volunteers expand as well.

PRAY

In Matthew 9, Jesus saw the crowds of people who needed to experience His love. Notice what He says.

"Jesus went through all the towns and villages, teaching in their synagogues, proclaiming the good news of the kingdom and healing every disease and sickness. When He saw the crowds, He had compassion on them, because they were harassed and helpless, like sheep without a shepherd. Then He said to His disciples, 'The harvest is plentiful but the workers are few. Ask the Lord of the harvest, therefore, to send out workers into His harvest field'."
Matthew 9:35-38[24]

Praying is crucial in building a great volunteer team. Jesus says if you need more volunteers, then ask God for them. He wouldn't tell you to ask for something, He didn't want to give you. Yes, God expects you to do your part and ask people. But as mentioned earlier, when we talked about divine appointments, prayer makes the difference when you ask people to volunteer.

What if you could have every volunteer you ever wanted? I mean, you had so many volunteers that you had to create a waiting list. I believe it can happen when your ministry is anointed with the power of prayer. Do this. Make a list of every volunteer role you need for your ministry. Better yet, expand the list by adding every single volunteer role you would want if you had an unlimited number of volunteers. Turn that list into a prayer list. Ask God every day to send the right people to fill those roles. And watch Him use you and your team make it become a reality.

Talk About It...

Do we see volunteers with an Ephesians 4 perspective?

Are we inviting to the "why" over the "what?"

Do we have a clearly stated, big vision that people want to give their best to? How can we communicate it more effectively?

Do people perceive our ministry as the Titanic or a Carnival cruise ship? Are there any changes we need to make?

Are we intentional about providing one-time serving opportunities with the intention that we will ask them to join our team on a regular basis? How can we improve this?

Where are the hot spots in our ministry?

Do we have an "every member serves" expectation and culture? How can we implement this or improve this?

Are we giving kids, students, families and senior adults the opportunity to serve? How can we improve with each of these age groups?

Are we intentional about asking current volunteers to invite other people to serve with them?

What are our entry level volunteer opportunities? What are some new serving roles we can create that would attract new volunteers?

Do we have a "dream list" of volunteers? If not, should we make one and use it as a prayer guide and invite reminder?

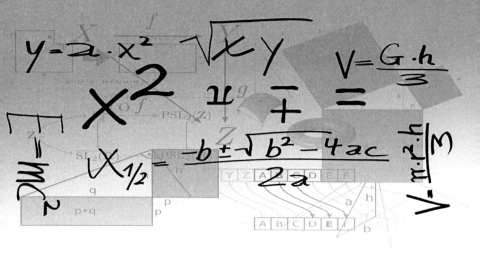

Action Steps

1.

2.

3.

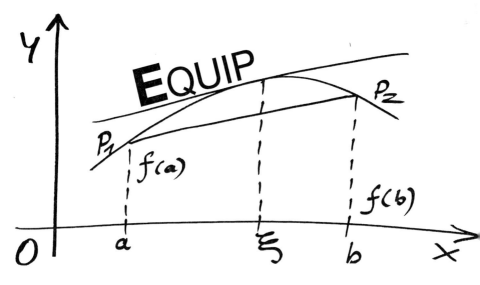

Imagine this. You get a call from a NFL football team. They want you to join their team. Stuttering in disbelief, you try to tell them you don't have that kind of experience, but they say, "Don't worry about it! You'll be fine! We'll take care of you. We need you on our team and we'll give you an out-of-this-world salary if you say 'yes.'" Well, even though you're leery about it, you agree. They tell you that your first day will be September 12 and to show up at 1:00 pm. You ask when training camp and practice will be, but they tell you to just show up on the 12th and they'll take good care of you. You show up on the 12th and it's not a practice field! It's a stadium filled with tens of thousands of excited people! Their cheering is deafening! This is no practice! It's game time! You head to the locker room to meet with the rest of your team, only to find out they're already out on the sideline. They forgot to tell you what time the pre-game meeting started.

You rush out to the field and join the team on the sideline just as the last few words of the national anthem are being sung. The coach spots you and motions for you to come to him. To your shock, he tells you that you'll be playing quarterback today. Exasperated, you tell him you've never played that position and are not prepared. And you remind him that you still haven't been given your helmet, pads and uniform. Without this preparation and protection, you tell him you'll get demolished out there! He looks at you, smiles and says, "Don't worry about it! You'll be fine! Now get in there! I need you in that position! There's no one else available! If you don't play, we'll have to forfeit the game. Needless to say, the game doesn't go well for you!

Now we know this would never happen in real life. Before a player ever steps on an NFL football field, they have been given the training, practice, resources, equipment and coaching they need to be successful.

But the sad truth is, this often happens to volunteers in ministry. We quickly sign them up, promise them a huge "payday" in heaven and then shove them in a position with no training, equipment or know how. And then we wonder why they struggle, burn out and quit.

You think it would be tough facing a football team unprepared and unequipped? *Try facing a room full of pre-schoolers unprepared and unequipped!*

Football players smell after a game...ever smell a preschooler after an accident?

Football players hit hard...preschoolers bite hard.

Football players begin running out of energy in the 4th quarter...preschoolers never run out of energy.

Football players yell in warm-ups...preschoolers yell so loud you can hear them over 200 adults in a crowded restaurant.

Football players eat protein bars...preschoolers eat glue sticks and crayons.

Football players hide family secrets...preschoolers tell family secrets.

Football players throw passes...preschoolers throw tantrums.

Football players aren't always brave enough to say what they're thinking...preschoolers always say what they're thinking.

Football players ask questions about plays...preschoolers ask questions about everything.

All kidding aside, it's critical that you provide new volunteers with training for their role. Enlist is all about bringing people on your team. **Equip is the next step and it's all about setting volunteers up for success by providing them with the knowledge, resources and tools they need.** Let's jump into this.

DOER VS. EQUIPPER

*"Their responsibility is to **EQUIP** God's people to do His work and build up the church, the body of Christ."*
Ephesians 4:12[1]

As a leader, you are called to be an equipper. Your job is not to do the work of the ministry, but to equip others to do the work of the ministry. Ephesians 4 is very clear about this.

EQUIPPING FROM THE START

"Training should not be seen as optional; rather, it should be operationalized and embedded into the fabric of your organization."
Jeff James, Vice President & General Manager of Disney Institute[2]

Equipping must start from the very beginning when you are bringing a new volunteer on the team. How you bring new volunteers on the team sets the tone for their entire serving experience. Let's talk about how equipping can be embedded in the onboarding process.

Onboarding Process for a New Volunteer:
Step 1 - Interest card filled out
Step 2 - Application filled out
Step 3 - Interview
Step 4 - Background check and reference calls
Step 5 - Orientation
Step 6 - On-the-job training

Step 1 – Interest card:
• Simple card that you use to capture basic contact information for potential volunteers such as name, email and phone number.

Step 2- Application:
• Application filled out to apply for serving. Should include permission for background check.
• You can get a sample of an application at www.buildingchildrensministry.com. The application can be hard copy or online.
• Should include providing a personality test, spiritual gifts test and a list of serving opportunities.

Step 3 – Personal interview:

- Look over the person's application before you meet with them and make a note of anything that could be a red flag.
- Sit down with the person and go over the interview questions. You can get a list of interview questions at www.buildingchildrensministry.com.
- If the person reveals any major red flags that will prevent him or her from serving in a specific area like children's ministry, address those concerns. On the next page are some tips for this:
- Be pro-active and ask the person if anything is going to pop on their background check that might hinder them from serving.

> If a person has abused a child, they should not be allowed to serve in children's ministry. Not now. Not ever.

> If it is a case of past addictions, such as drugs or alcohol, have a set time frame that they must have been free from the addiction. This could be 2 years, 3 years, etc. This is something your ministry must decide on.

> Don't make the decision alone. Have a team of people who work together to decide if a red flag will disqualify the person from serving.

> If the person cannot serve in a specific area due to a red flag, then use it as a shepherding and ministry opportunity. Let's pause to talk about that for a moment.

When the interview, background check or another part of the onboarding process produces a red flag, how do you guide this difficult conversation? Here are some steps.

Affirm the person as a part of your church family. Start off by sharing with them how much you love them and that you are thankful they are part of your church family. Share with them how much you appreciate them wanting to serve.

Explain that a red flag popped while taking them through the process. Share with them what it was. (examples...a drug use conviction a year ago, reference call information, application, answers to questions, etc.).

Ask them to share more about the "red flag." It's important to allow them to explain what happened. This is not so they can talk you into letting them serve, but to hear their heart and journey so you can help them move forward.

Explain the "why" of the process. Share that it's nothing personal against them, but rather a system you have in place to ensure the safety and security of the children or other area they cannot serve in. Share that you go the second mile to accomplish this, hence you have very high standards in place.

Be a shepherd. More than likely they are going to feel either anger, hurt, sadness or guilt. They may even question if you want them to be part of the church family.

This is such a key time in the conversation. Again, affirm how much you love them. Share with them how thankful you are that they are part of the church family.

Provide them with next steps. Don't leave them hanging. This is one of the most critical times of the conversation. God is giving you the opportunity to help this person grow in their relationship with Him. Give them next steps they can take to continue to grow spiritually. Perhaps it's a class or program they can be part of. Perhaps it's another ministry in the church where they can serve that doesn't require as high of standards. Follow up and help them get connected.

Let them know "no" now doesn't mean "no" indefinitely. Share with them that when the red flag is removed you'd like to have them as part of the team one day (example - if you have a 2-year wait process for someone who had a drug conviction). As previously stated, the exception would be someone who has abused a child wanting to serve in children's ministry. That would be a permanent red flag.

Asking the hard questions and having those kinds of conversations are not easy, but it must be done. Remember, it's nobody's right to serve. It's a privilege. Especially when it comes to serving with children. Children's safety and security must come before anyone's feelings.

- Talk with the person about their personality, spiritual gifts and passion. This will help you guide them into the right serving role. We'll talk more in-depth about that in a moment.
- If the person is a good fit for the team, then let them know you will run the background check and if no other conversations are needed after the background check, they will receive an invitation to an orientation. If they are not a good fit or cannot serve in your area, then follow the shepherding steps above.

- Close the interview with prayer.
- If you know there are going to be some red flags and you're going to need to have a hard conversation, it's best to have another person with you during the interview as a witness. You will also need to go back and write down what was said on the interview form to have on record.
- It is best to have males interview males and females interview females due to the nature of some of the questions you are asking.
- Some questions are only asked to people 18 and over. And anyone under 18 should have his or her parent present for the interview.

Step 4 – Background check:
- Run a background check on everyone over the age of 17. Let me repeat that. Everyone. No exceptions.
- As stated above, if the background check has no red flags, then you can invite the person to your next orientation.
- If a red flag does pop on the background check, then you'll need to follow the plan previously mentioned.

Step 5 – Orientation:
- This is the last step to becoming an official member of the team.
- Once a person's background check is clear, they are invited to the orientation.
- Orientation should be the 30,000 ft. view of the ministry. Here's some of the things you'll want to cover.

    Have everyone introduce themselves.

    History of the ministry.

    Vision of the ministry (the ministry leader should be the one to cast this vision either in person or by video).

Core values of the ministry.

Ministry philosophy.

Essential safety and security procedures.

General expectations such as being on time, being prepared, attire, what to do if need to be absent, etc.

Benefits of serving. Here's an example of what I've used for this in a children's ministry orientation.

- First of all, you're joining a **FAMILY**. You're going to find you develop friendships with the people you serve with. You'll laugh together, share prayer requests, support each other, pray for each other and encourage each other. You see, we weren't meant to do the Christian life alone…and serving in this ministry means you will be surrounded by friends who will walk with you on your journey. You're gaining a family.

- You're also getting ready to be a part of **FUN**. Yes…that's right! Fun! And lots of it. No matter your age…there's still a little kid inside you who wants to have fun. And now that you're a part of our team…you can let that little kid out and have fun. Laugh…smile...enjoy yourself. Have a good time!

- Another benefit of serving in our ministry is **FAITH**. You're going to find your faith growing. You see, serving is a key component of growing your faith. So, get ready to see your spiritual growth accelerate as you begin serving.

- There's something else you're going to be part of by joining the team…and that's a **FOCUS**. We are focused on one thing – impacting our world with the love and message of Jesus…everyone...everyday...everywhere.

This is **WHY** you will be serving. This is why you will be holding babies in the nursery. Why you will be helping preschoolers color a Bible story picture. Why you will be greeting new kids and families. Why you will be leading a group of kids. Why you will be running a computer presentation or sound board. Why you will be passing out take-home papers. Why you will be helping families check in. Why you will be leading kids in worship. Why you will be sharing a Bible story. Why you will be helping keep the kids safe. It's so they can be impacted by the love and message of Jesus Christ and discover the hope that's found in Him. This is the focus of the team you are joining. It's a focus that's worth giving your best to.

- You're also going to experience **FULLNESS** of joy. There is a joy that comes from serving others. It's a deep, abiding joy that comes from knowing God is using your life to help other people. You're going to discover it truly is more joyful to give than to receive. As you give yourself away…your joy will be full.

- And finally, you are going to be a part of **FRUIT**. The Bible tells us as Christians, we are to bear fruit. By fruit, it means helping other people come to Christ. And you picked a great ministry to bear fruit. Did you know that 85% of people who come to Christ do so before the age of 18? I believe the heart of a child is the most fertile soil in which to plant the Word of God. Studies show children learn more in their early years than at any other time in life. You're going to see spiritual fruit. You're going to see kids step across the line of faith and become lifelong followers of Christ. You're going to see kids immediately grab hold of what you share and begin to live it out. And not only will you see the fruit now…but later as well as your ministry continues to bear fruit in their lives as they grow up.

So, get ready to experience family…fun...your faith growing…focus that matters…fullness of joy and lots of fruit.

Again, this was written from the perspective of serving in children's ministry. Whichever ministry you're representing in the orientation, make sure you bring passion and vision and purpose. Remember, this will set the tone for their serving experience with the team.

Step 6 – On-the-job training:

- Coming out of orientation, place volunteers in the area they will be serving for on-the-job training.
- The length of the training will depend on the role. Some roles will require more training than others.
- Place the new volunteer with an experienced volunteer that they can shadow. Here's an example for on-the-job training for a small group leader.

  Week 1 – observe a group

  Week 2 – co-lead a group

  Week 3 – lead a group with the veteran observing and giving feedback

  Week 4 – lead own group

SWEET SPOT

I believe that one of the biggest factors in equipping a new volunteer and setting them up for success is helping them find their sweet spot. In other words, placing them in a role that aligns with their personality, gifting and passion.

Normally, when you ask a new volunteer where they want to serve, they will say, "Wherever you need me." The temptation is to place them where you have a need. You feel the pressure of the need and see an opportunity to fill it quickly...whether the person is a fit or not. But resist the temptation. Take the long look. If you place the person in the "need" and it's not their passion or area of giftedness, you will eventually lose them.

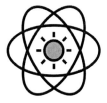

"Don't place people where you need them.
Place people where they need to be!"

Where do they need to be? Let me say it again for emphasis. They need to be in a role that aligns with their personality, gifts and passion. I remember a few years ago, I was excited about a new volunteer who was coming on board. When I sat down to interview him, I asked him where he was interested in serving. He said, "I saw on the list of opportunities that you have a 4th grade boys' small group leader role. I am willing to do that." Inside, I was like "Yes! We need some boys' small group leaders! That's where I'm putting him." But before I said those words, I knew I needed to ask him one more question. I said, "That's great. But let me ask you a question. If you could serve anywhere in the church, where would that be? What is your dream job at church?" He paused and then said, "Well, to be honest, I love working with high school students. That's my first passion. But I know you could use some more 4th grade small group leaders, so that's what I'm going to do." As much as I wanted to say, "Okay," I couldn't. I would have been doing him a disservice and he wouldn't have been fulfilled. So, biting my tongue, I said, "As much as I'd like to have you leading a 4th grade boys' small group, I'm going to have to say 'no.' Come with me. I'm going to take you over and introduce you to our high school pastor. That's your sweet spot. That's where you need to be."

Remember, it's not about using the person to fill a spot. It's about helping them discover the gifts and talents God has placed in them and seeing them walk in those gifts. When this happens, they will thrive! When this happens, they will love what they are doing! When this happens, they will stick around!

I often tell new volunteers, if you are in your sweet spot, you will go home energized by serving. Sure, we all have days when we are tired and not jumping for joy, but overall you will have an abiding sense of joy and fulfillment when you are in your sweet spot. But when a person is not in their sweet spot, they dread serving and go home drained from it. Most people who are not in their sweet spot end up quitting or if they have a lot of character, they stick it out, but serve out of duty and not delight. A big part of your job, as an equipper, is helping people find their sweet spot. Here are some keys to doing this.

Give them a personality test. Each role in your ministry will appeal to a certain personality type. And you want to match up the right personalities with the corresponding roles. An example would someone who is an extrovert. They would

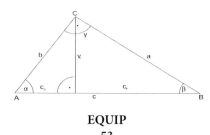

probably be a good fit for a greeter role.

Give them a spiritual gifts test. Again, each role in your ministry will line up with a spiritual gift. And you want to put people in roles that align with their spiritual gifts. An example would be someone who has the gift of hospitality. They would probably be a good fit for helping prepare and serve snacks.

*A helpful way to do this is to list which personality traits and spiritual gifts align with each role.

Ask key questions when you interview them.
- Have you served in a ministry in the past?
  (if yes, explain more)
- What do you enjoy doing?
- What are you hoping to offer the people you serve?
- Are there any special skills or talents you could bring to the team?
- What would be your dream role at church?
- What excites you most about serving?
- Do you feel drawn toward a specific role?

Provide them with guidance as needed. Sometimes a person's perception of what they are gifted at may not line up with reality. Or their passion may not line up with their giftedness. A person's sweet spot involves both passion and giftedness. I can say I have the gift of singing, but if I tried to lead worship, people would probably run out the back door. I can carry a tune, but it somehow gets lost when I try to unload it. If I told someone I wanted to lead worship, I hope they would care enough to help guide me to my true areas of giftedness. And there will be times when a new volunteer has a gift, but needs more time to develop it. An example is someone who wants to jump in and teach a class, but needs more coaching and training before they are ready.

While we are on this subject, let me ask you a question. Do you have volunteers who are serving in roles that don't line up with their gifting and personality? Is it hindering the ministry because no one wants to "hurt" the person's feelings by redirecting them? The truth is, leaving the person in that role is not only hurting the ministry, but them as well. Is it time to have the conversation with a volunteer that you know you need to have?

Years ago, I came into a ministry as the new children's ministry leader and quickly discovered that the lady who was the primary greeter, was not in her sweet spot. She had the personality of the Wicked Witch of the West and was rude and abrupt with families. Somewhere back there someone had placed her in the wrong role. And so, I had to sit down with her and explain that we'd like her to serve in a different role. It wasn't an easy conversation, but it was a necessary conversation. Are there some people in your ministry that are serving in the wrong role that you need to move?

Let them observe several areas if they are undecided. Sometimes a new volunteer will come out of the interview and orientation still undecided where their sweet spot is. They may have more than one role they feel drawn toward. Encourage them to observe several areas as part of the decision-making process.

Give them permission to let you know if they are not in their sweet spot. Sometimes a person will get in a role and realize after a few weeks that it's not the right fit after all. Let them know up front that if this happens, to let you know so you can help them find a role that is a better fit.

Check back with them one month after they start serving to see if they are in their sweet spot. Don't wait for them to approach you. A month after they start serving, sit down with them and ask if they are in their sweet spot. If they are not, encourage them to try a different role. When people are in their sweet spot, great things happen!

I first noticed Len when I saw kids flocking to him after the service and parents bringing their kids to see him. He was a kid-magnet. I thought, "I've got to get to know this guy." The reason kids flocked to Len was because he looks just like Santa Claus. As I got to know him, I found out he actually plays Santa Claus at Christmas in major department stores like Macy's across the country. As we invited Len to join our volunteer team, we shared with him our vision of having a Disney-like "mayor" character in costume for our children's building. It was the perfect spot for Len and he gladly said "yes." As mayor of our children's ministry, Len would greet kids as they entered while donning his mayor costume. He looked like he'd just stepped out of a Disney movie. Kids would come running to see him. He brought so many smiles to kids and families. Len is in his 70's and has shared with us how serving in this role has brought new joy and purpose to his life. That's what happens when someone serves in his or her sweet spot.

Dwight is a successful businessman who serves in our ministry. When I met with him about which role he could serve in, I already had in mind where I thought he should serve. A former college football player and strong leader, I thought he would be a perfect fit to lead one of our boys' groups. We have many boys who come from single parent households and I thought he would be a great mentor and role model for a group of them. He had been looking over the list of serving opportunities and so when we met, I was hoping and praying he would say, "I want to lead a small group of boys."

"Well, Dwight," I said, "You've looked at and prayed over the list of serving opportunities. Where do you feel you would be a good fit?" His response took me by surprise. "Dale," he said, "I've been praying about this and I believe God wants me to serve in the...nursery." I grinned and said, "The nursery? Are you sure?" He said, "Yes, I have a soft spot in my heart for babies. As you know, my wife and I have kids that are in elementary school now. We miss having babies around. I believe I'd like to serve in the nursery and help with the babies."

I could have pushed back and probably made the case for Dwight being a boys' small group leader...and he probably would have said "okay" and served with the boys. He has that kind of servant's heart. But...he wouldn't have been in his sweet spot.

You see, now Dwight is known in our nursery as the "baby whisperer." That's right. Anytime there's a baby crying, we bring the little one to Dwight. He takes the baby in his big arms and gently whispers and rocks the little one into a peaceful state. He is one of our best nursery volunteers. And he loves it. As I said, he is a successful businessman and recently he was in Chicago for business. He realized he had signed up to serve in the nursery for the Saturday night service. He hopped on a plane that morning. Flew from Chicago to south Florida. Served in the nursery. After serving, he got back on a plane and flew back to his work in Chicago. What would cause a person to be that committed? It comes from being in your sweet spot.

- When someone is in their sweet spot, it energizes them.
- When someone is in their sweet spot, they love it.
- When someone is in their sweet spot, the role comes naturally for them.
- When someone is in their sweet spot, they bear fruit.
- When someone is in their sweet spot, they thrive.
- When someone is in their sweet spot, they last.

PROVIDE A JOB DESCRIPTION

Check out these humorous job descriptions:

Shows you innovative ways to burn money in the spirit of patriotism. (Fireworks Stand Manager)

Go to strange people's houses and take their money. (Pizza Delivery Person)

Take pictures of the unlucky and the stupid. (X-ray Technician)

Have people spend far more than they estimated. (Building Inspector)

Make sure nothing ever happens. (IT Security)

Copy and paste the Internet. (Student)

Stand on a field and get yelled at for hours. (Baseball Umpire)

Talk in other people's sleep. (College Professor)

Run away and call the police. (Security Guard)

In all seriousness, if you want to set your volunteers up for success, it's vital to equip them with a clear job description. You can't hold someone accountable if they don't know what they are supposed to do. Here are some key things to include in the job description.

- Overview & Purpose of the role.

- Time commitment.

- Who they report to.

- General expectations – be on time, informing when you're going to be absent, attend training, etc.

- Specific expectations – prepare crafts, pass out bulletins, run stage lights, etc.

- What spiritual gifts and personality traits are needed for the position.

- What the wins are for the position (what success practically looks like).

On the next few pages is a sample of a job description. You can get a complete set of children's ministry job descriptions at www.buildingchildrensministry.com.

Children's Ministry Large Group Teacher

Role Description:
As a large group teacher, you will have the opportunity to communicate the Bible story during weekend services in a creative and interactive way so that it captures the attention of every child and is planted in their heart.

Ministry Areas:
- Preschool
- Elementary

Serving Time:
• Weekday lesson prep time.
• Serve during scheduled weekend service.
• Arrival time for serving is 45 minutes prior to start of service. End time is approximately 20 minutes after the service.

Responsibilities:
• Work with other large group volunteers (i.e. host, game leaders, worship leaders, etc.) to effectively deliver the teaching elements in alignment with the curriculum.
• Learn lesson materials to effectively present the Bible teaching in a creative and memorable way.
• Attend pre-service huddle with your team.
• Attend mid-week rehearsal as scheduled.
• Invite other people to join the team and serve alongside you.

Requirements:
• Ability to effectively communicate with kids and teach the Bible story in a fun, creative and memorable way.
• Everyone over the age of 17 must have a completed background check on file and must have completed the interview and orientation process to serve.
• Encouraged to attend new member's class.

Role is best suited for a person with these spiritual gifts:
Teaching, wisdom, knowledge and exhortation.

Role is best suited for someone with this personality:
Energetic, fun and outgoing.

Wins for This Role:
• Kids are engaged with the lesson.
• Kids can remember the key teaching point from the lesson.
• Kids look forward to the lesson time.

After meeting the requirements above, you will be paired up with an experienced leader who will guide and mentor you while providing on-the-job-training.

Sit down with the new volunteer and go over the role description with him or her before they start serving so they have a clear understanding of what they will be doing.

RESOURCES

What supplies will the volunteer need? How will the curriculum be delivered to them when they are teaching? Who do they go to if they run out of something? These may seem like small details, but they are big to a new volunteer coming in. The better you prepare them, the more confident they will be starting in their new role and the more successful they will be.

Think about it like this. Let's go back to the football analogy. If a quarterback throws a pass at the receiver's feet, the receiver might still make the catch, but it's difficult. But if the quarterback throws it right on target, in the receiver's chest area, the receiver is a lot more likely to make the catch.

When you provide a new volunteer with the resources and preparation, he or she needs, you are throwing them a ball that is easily catchable. But when you don't give them what they need, it's like you're throwing the ball at their feet.

"Great leaders set their volunteers up for success by throwing them a pass that is easy to catch."

ONE-ON-ONE MENTORING

We have talked about providing on-the-job training. I believe it is the most effective way to train new volunteers. Most of what we learn is through watching others. But to be prepared for this, you need to have some veteran volunteers that can serve as mentors to new volunteers. You need to have some Pauls ready for the Timothys to shadow. Take a few minutes and write down the names of some of your Pauls (and Mrs. Pauls) below who could serve as mentors for new volunteers.

1.
2.
3.
4.

The next step is to approach these key volunteers and ask them if they will serve as mentors to new volunteers. Share with them the opportunity they have to multiply their leadership and influence by mentoring new volunteers.

When I first started serving in children's ministry as a teenager, I was mentored by a man named Jerry. Each week, I went with Jerry to visit kids and invite them to church. Jerry drove an old pick-up truck. The first week I went visiting the kids with him in the old truck, we got to the first house and he said, "We've got to find an incline to park on." I thought that was odd. After we were done visiting the family, I found out why. The starter in that old truck often acted up and instead of getting it fixed, he just parked on an incline and started it by popping the clutch while it was rolling. And when we were at a house with no incline to be found, guess who had to push the truck so he could pop the clutch? Yours truly.

Jerry's old truck may not have been the best, but he taught me how to care about kids and families. He taught me to be faithful. He taught me how important it is to share your faith with people who don't know Jesus. He taught me how to get kids excited about coming to church. He taught me to give my best as a volunteer. I'm thankful for the investment Jerry made in my life as a young volunteer. You have some Jerrys in your ministry. Ask them to help you equip the new volunteers that God brings into your ministry.

ONGOING TRAINING STRATEGIES

We've talked about the initial equipping that is needed as you bring new volunteers on your team. Now let's talk about ongoing training strategies. **Effective training is not one and done. It is ongoing with a clear strategy to help volunteers continue to grow as Christ-followers and leaders in ministry.**

As you think about your ongoing training, here are some questions to consider.

- How often will we provide training?
- What specific topics does the team need training in?
- How will we get people to attend?
- What platform will we use to bring the training?
- What elements need to be part of the training?
- What format will we use?

There are also some factors to keep in mind as you plan your training strategy.

Volunteers are busy. The pace of life is faster than ever. Here's an example. Do you ever find yourself intensely scanning the check-out lines at Target to make sure you get in the shortest line? Then when you're in that line, you watch the other lines to see if any of them are moving faster than yours. And if a line does move faster, you kick yourself for not getting in that line!

Parents are working an average of 11 more hours a week than they did in the 1970's.[3] Family vacations? On the average, families are taking a week less than they did in 2000. In fact, 42% of adults say they have not taken a single day off in the past year.[4] 22% of parents say it's been over a year since their last family vacation.[5] It's obvious that in such a busy culture, volunteers consider their time one of their most valuable commodities and they are only going to give you so much of it.

Volunteers are bombarded with lots of information. Between commercials, print ads, radio ads, Facebook ads, Google ads, ads on smart phones and everything else an ad can be put on, we are exposed to hundreds of messages each day. All of this creates a noise…a buzz…that you have to somehow find a way to get your message to rise above and be heard through.

Volunteers have short attention spans. The attention span is an endangered species in the lightning-fast, multi-media society we've become. With media overload continuing to amp up, the ability to capture volunteers' attention and hold it, is an increasing challenge.

New research finds that the average political sound byte, defined as any footage of a candidate speaking uninterrupted - has dropped to just 8 seconds. To give that information some context, consider that, during the 1968 presidential election, the average sound byte was a full 43 seconds. And as recently as the 1990s, CBS said it wouldn't broadcast any sound byte under 30 seconds in an effort to better promote informed, complex discourse.[6]

According to the Pediatrics medical journal, increased exposure to television and video games has caused noticeable decreases in attention spans. One study revealed the average attention span of university students is 8 to 10 minutes.[7] We have to keep this in mind as we prepare our training. Due to shrinking attentions spans, there are 3 words you will hear more often. They are, "It's too long."

"That training video…it's too long."

"That teaching…it's too long."

"That email…it's too long."

"That class…it's too long."

With these factors in mind, here are some ongoing training strategies that can help you be effective.

LIVE TRAINING EVENTS

When you do live training events, make the time you have it as convenient as possible. The more convenient it is for people to attend, the better your attendance will be. I have found that usually the best time to have live training is when volunteers are already going to be at church. Here are some options for this.

- Option 1 – If you have multiple services, offer it during each service hour. This allows volunteers to serve one hour and attend training the other hour.

- Option 2 – Have it right after the last service is over.

- Option 3 – Have it during the time they are normally serving. Bring in a special guest or get substitutes to teach the kids. This not only gives every volunteer the opportunity to attend training, but gives them a week off as well. And it guarantees 90-100% volunteer attendance.

For live training events, less is more. I remember when I first started in ministry, I would hold weekly volunteer meetings that were an hour long. But that was over 20 years ago and even back then it was too much. Over the years, I have shifted to having live training events just three times a year. **One in February to prepare the team for the spring ministry season, one in August to prepare the team for the fall ministry season and one in early November to help the team finish the year strong.** These training events are normally an hour long.

When you have live training events, make it worth their time. Someone said the reason people don't attend volunteer training events is because they have been before.

As I have led volunteer training over the past 27 years, I've had some trainings that were a success and others that were a failure, some were home runs and some were strikeouts, some were memorable and some needed to be forgotten, some were energizing and some were blah.

Through trial and error, I have found 7 key elements that make up effective volunteer training. None of these stand alone. It takes all 7 to make it rock. Incorporate these into your training and you will see great results.

#1 - Fun. There should be laughter. Lots of it. This can be done through funny skits, games, jokes, videos, etc.

#2 - Festive. Make it a party. Decorate with a theme. Play music when they are arriving. Give away door prizes.

#3 - Food. Serving food shows your volunteers you value them. Plus, it's hard for people to focus on training if their stomachs are growling.

#4 - Family-Friendly. Provide childcare and food for their children. Avoid having the training on a school night.

#5 - Focused. Be prepared. Know exactly what the agenda is and what you are going to cover.

#6 - Faith-Building. Remember, we are called to make disciples. The training should not only help them grow in their ministry skills, but in their faith as well. One goal of the training should be to deepen their walk with Christ.

#7 - Felt. There should be a moment that is memorable and leaves a tear in their eyes. An "ah ha" moment. Remind them of why they serve. Encourage them. Thank them for the difference they are making. If possible, give them a small gift to express your appreciation.

Offer specific training as needed. There will be times when you need to hold smaller trainings for a specific group of volunteers.

PRE-SERVICE HUDDLES

A pre-service huddle is a great way to invest in your volunteers and provide quick, weekly training. This is done by meeting with your volunteers an extra 15 minutes right before they are scheduled to start serving. An example would be meeting at 9:45 am with your volunteers who are scheduled to start serving at 10:00 a.m.

If you will be intentional with this time, it can be a catalyst for your team. Here are elements I include when leading a pre-service huddle.

Laughter (1 min.)
Share a funny story, joke or video.

Recognition (1 min.)
• Introduce any new team members.
• Honor one of your volunteers and give him/her a small gift.

Announcements (1 min.)
Share any important information volunteers need to know.

Teaching (5 min.)
Rotate through 3 different teaching topics. One topic per week.
 •Practical - help them grow in their ministry skills.
 •Devotional - help them grow spiritually.
 •Motivational - help grow their passion for ministry.

Care (3 min.)
Give volunteers the opportunity to share prayer requests & personal needs.

Prayer (3 min.)
Spend time praying for the volunteers' needs and for the ministry.

DNA Infusion (1 min.)
Have everyone repeat the mission statement or one of the core values. Say it as a cheer to make it fun.

Total - 15 minutes

Just think, if you're intentional with your pre-service huddles, you can provide 52 trainings in one year.

USING TECHNOLOGY FOR TRAINING

In today's connected world, online training is a great tool to use. Rather than always trying to drag volunteers to your training, why not take the training to your volunteers? Your volunteers are already online. Go where they are.

The ability to create training videos is in the palm of your hand. It's as simple as grabbing your smartphone, recording a training, uploading it to a site like YouTube or

Vimeo (or the latest, greatest video site) and sending the link to your volunteers to watch. This enables volunteers to access the training at any time.

Use social media for training. Your volunteers are on social media sites and apps like Facebook, Twitter and Instagram (or the latest, greatest social media tool). An example is creating a Facebook page for your volunteers and using Facebook Live for training. The video will post once you are done as well for later viewing.

Keep it short. Remember that your volunteers' attention spans are short. They are probably not going to watch a 15-minute training video. Keep your videos to 2-3 minutes.

Use technology for updates and communication. Want to make sure your volunteers understand how to lead the craft time this coming weekend? Need to walk them through an activity they'll be doing with the kids? Got some important announcements you need to make sure they know about? Grab your smart phone, record a short video and send it to them. As technology continues to rapidly advance, it provides many opportunities to take training to your volunteers.

EQUIPPING MILLENNIALS

We talked briefly about Millennials and what it takes to bring them on your team in the first chapter. When it comes to equipping them, you need to know what makes them tick as well.

Millennials want to be developed as leaders. They are looking for opportunities to grow and develop the gifts, talents and passions God has placed in them.

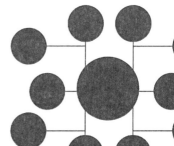

Millennials are looking for a coach. They are not going to follow title alone. They are going to follow someone who will value them as a person and invest in them. They are looking for someone who can help them understand and build their gifts and talents.

Millennials don't want to fix their weaknesses...they want to develop their strengths. Research has shown that weaknesses never develop into strengths, while strengths can develop infinitely. This means if you want to keep Millennial volunteers, it's critical that you place them in their area of giftedness and help them continually grow and thrive in that area.

BE AN EQUIPPER

There are always lots of ministry tasks that need to be accomplished, aren't there? So, what do we do? We get busy and we get it done...even if it means working extra hours, missing some sleep, or sacrificing in other areas of our life. We get things done…no matter what it takes. And in the process, we shortchange ourselves, our volunteers and the ministry. Yes, often it's easier and quicker to just do it ourselves. But we must take the long look and equip others to do the work of the ministry.

"You can go faster alone…
but you can go farther together."

In the long run, switching to being an equipper will result in a much stronger, healthier ministry. And it will enable the ministry to be sustainable and accomplish so much more than you could have done by yourself.

Talk About It...

Do we have a clear on-boarding process for new volunteers? How can we improve this?

Are we placing people in their sweet spot? How can we improve this?

Do we provide new volunteers with a job description?

Are we hitting new volunteers between the numbers with the ball or throwing it at their feet? How can we do a better job at setting them up for success?

Do our new volunteers know what the wins are for their role? How can we make the wins clearer for them?

Are we using a pre-service huddle to equip volunteers? How can we be more intentional with this?

What is our ongoing training strategy? Is it effective? Are the trainings well attended? How can we improve this?

How are we using technology to equip volunteers? How can we use technology more effectively?

Do Millennial volunteers see us as a coach? How can we focus more on helping them develop their strengths?

As leaders, are we spending more time doing or equipping? How can we become better equippers?

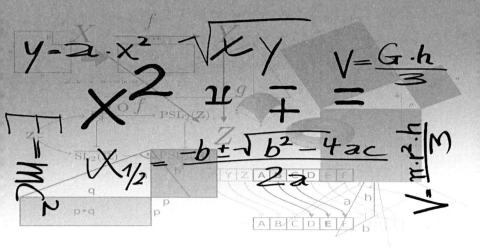

Action Steps

1.

2.

3.

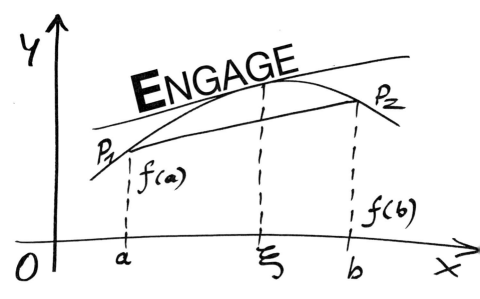

Enlist is how you bring new volunteers on the team. Equip is how you set volunteers up for success. **Engage is how you keep volunteers on the team. It's about engaging volunteers through meaningful relationships.**

"How long people serve is in direct correlation to the depth of the relationships they form with the people they serve with."

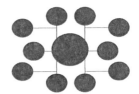

People are lonely. Reports say an unprecedented number of people have less and less connection to close friends and family. Families have fewer family outings and share fewer family dinners together.

In every church, people are looking for ways to get connected with other believers. And one of the best ways to establish relationships is through serving. Perhaps we'd have more people join our volunteer teams if we stopped telling them how much help we need and start telling them serving is the best place to get connected and form relationships.

Relationships form and flourish in a culture of FAITH.

Remember what we talked about in Enlist? The foundation of serving is discipleship. When volunteers come together with a sense of spiritual calling and purpose, it unites them in relationship. And when volunteers see serving as a way to encourage and help each other grow spiritually, it deepens their relationship.

Take time to get volunteers together for prayer each week before they serve. We talked about this in the previous chapter under the huddle section. Be intentional about giving volunteers time to share prayer requests and pray for each other.

"Volunteers who pray together grow in relationship together."

Form small groups and Bible studies with volunteers. Actively encourage volunteers to get in a group together. Set the example by leading a group yourself.

Encourage volunteers to worship together. When you see volunteers sitting in worship together, it is a great indicator that relationships are being formed.

Group volunteers together by spiritual gifting and passion. This goes back to placing people in their sweet spot. When you group people together who have the same spiritual gifts, they will naturally begin to bond. Tech guys will bond around their love for computers. People who love babies will bond around babies. People who love to lead kids in worship will bond around that. People who love to lead small groups of kids will enjoy serving with other people who love to do the same.

Relationships form and flourish in a culture of FAMILY.

Be intentional about creating a "family" atmosphere. When volunteers feel they are part of a family that knows them, loves them and cares for them, they will last. Serving is about more than just teaching a class or greeting a family or helping park a car or preparing a craft. It's about doing life together. It's about having a family that will walk with you through the good times and the bad times.

Noemy directs the children's ministry at one of the campuses I oversaw. When you go to her campus, you immediately notice something. She has lots of volunteers on her team. Every room has plenty of people serving and they are happy to be there.

I asked her how she built such an amazing team. Her reply revealed the secret. She said, "I don't have volunteers... I have friends." Stop and think about that for a minute. What she was saying is she builds relationships with the people on her team. As she invests in them and cares for them, they become more than just someone filling a role. She engages them relationally. They become family.

Have volunteers over for a meal at your house or at a restaurant. Families eat together. If you want to immediately strengthen your relationship with a volunteer, then share a meal together.

Meet a volunteer for a cup of coffee. Use the time to get to know them better.

Form a group on social media. Start a Facebook or other social media group with your volunteer team.

Celebrate birthdays, anniversaries, births and other special life events. That's what family does.

Care for each other's needs. Family not only celebrates together; they support each other during tough times. Life brings not only mountaintops, but valleys as well. Volunteers will go through those valleys. But when they have a volunteer team around them that is truly functioning as a family, they will feel loved, supported and cared for during those times.

I'll never forget the heart-breaking tragedy one of our volunteers experienced. Her ex-husband was not a believer and made life difficult for her as a Christ-follower. They had two precious boys in grades 4 and 5. She was faithful to bring the boys to church and she served in preschool. Her ex-husband became increasingly antagonistic in her interactions with him. One day he showed up at the house and after entering, held her and the boys at gunpoint. He then proceeded to do the unthinkable in front of her. He took a rope out and strangled both boys to death while forcing her to watch. He said to her, "I'm not going to kill you because I want you to live with this the rest of your life." He then put the gun to his head and killed himself. There is no way to understand the deep pain, sorrow and grief this lady felt and continues to feel. But I have watched her volunteer family rally around her and provide prayer and support. She is still serving in preschool and though she will never completely get over this tragedy, she has survived with her faith in tact because of the volunteer family that supports her.

A culture of family is birthed when a team of volunteers commits to really knowing and understanding each other. Commit to moving beyond a shallow "how are you doing?" to really finding out how volunteers are doing. Ask them "how are you 'really' doing'?" Many times, volunteers won't share what's really going on in their life, unless you specifically ask them. Behind the smile may be suffering, depression, financial problems, family issues or other struggles.

Engaging in the small details of your volunteers' lives will allow you to make a big relational impact. It's the "little" things that show volunteers you care in a "big" way. *A great way to do this is to keep a favorites list for each volunteer.* This is a list of their favorites such as their favorite candy, favorite color, favorite movie, favorite restaurant, favorite snack, favorite drink, etc. You can then use this list to personally show them you care about them.

Commit to praying for each other. Share prayer requests, create a prayer chain and include prayer requests in your weekly communication.

Show volunteers that you care more about them as a person than about what they do for the ministry. Do your volunteers know you really care about them? I mean, really care?

I remember a few years ago, when one of our volunteers didn't show up to serve because his father had suddenly passed away. I decided to call and let him know we were praying for him and ask how we could help him during his time of loss.

When he picked up the phone, he immediately began to apologize for not being there to serve. I felt bad. His first thought was not, "Dale is calling because he cares about me and my family." His first thought was, "Dale is calling to see why I didn't show up for my role at church." I hadn't been providing the care and concern that he needed up to that point. Thankfully, I was able to change that and show him that I really cared. He is still serving to this day.

Do your volunteers really know you care about them? When the phone rings, is their first thought, "He or she is calling to see how I am doing?" or is it, "He or she is calling because they want something from me?"

"People don't follow a title.
They follow someone they know cares about them."

One of the best volunteer team builders I know is Lori. She was one of our staff members who oversaw the nursery. I learned a lot from her about building relationships with volunteers. Anytime I stopped by her nursery area, it was full of happy, smiling volunteers. That doesn't happen by accident. It comes from a leader who is building solid relationships with her volunteers. I asked her to share how she does this and here is what she told me.

Call your volunteers just to see how they are doing.

Thank each volunteer for serving every week.

Be aware that your volunteers have very busy lives. Things are going to happen. When they can't make it to serve, be understanding. *People respond better to grace than to pressure.*

Give your volunteers your personal cell phone number.

Be there to serve your volunteers. She sees herself as a flight attendant…going from room to room and meeting the needs of her team.

Get to know your volunteers personally. Know what is going on in their lives.

Show you care. She knows each volunteer's favorite treats and snacks. Each weekend, she bakes someone's favorite and brings it for them and the rest of the team.

Listen a lot more than you talk.

Connect your volunteers with each other. Help them build relationships with the people they serve with.

Make love a priority on your team. One of Lori's volunteers recently said she loves serving because it's the only place where she feels people love her for who she is.

Marni, who leads the preschool ministry at a campus I oversaw, is another great example of a leader who is creating a relational culture of family. I recently received this email from one of her volunteers.

"I wanted to take a moment and share something with you. I know as a business owner and a supervisor in the fire department, it is always nice to get a letter of appreciation for one of my team members. So what better day than today and today is her birthday. Although everyone on your team is awesome, I wanted to point out Marni. I have been serving with her in the kids' ministry for a couple years now and I have to say she demonstrates a lot of 'Christ-like love' to all the kids and her volunteers. Sometimes when I see her struggling to fill each room with enough volunteers for a Sunday service and she is short-handed, she never lets it get her down or change the way she treats people. Whenever I ask her about it, she always says 'it will all work out' of course with a smile. In my line of work, I pay people to come to work and when I can't fill my schedule I get frustrated. I've even gotten a little bit of an attitude. Well I have definitely changed my ways since observing how she treats people and also as I reflect on the Bible verse: Colossians 4:5-6 – 'Be wise in the way you act towards outsiders; make the most of every opportunity. Let your conversation be always full of grace, seasoned with salt, so that you may know how to answer everyone'."[3]

Here's what I learned from Marni about leading volunteers relationally:

The volunteer knows it's her birthday. *This means she leads on a personal level.*

He has been serving for 2 years. *She is keeping her volunteers because she is creating a culture of family.*

The volunteer is watching HOW she leads. *Volunteers observe how you lead.* Don't think they don't notice.

She doesn't get "stressed out" or at least she doesn't let it show. Want to see how your tone is? Look at the tone of your volunteers. *You set the tone for your volunteers.*

She has impacted this volunteer's life and helped him grow spiritually. *A good leader influences his or her volunteers spiritually.*

Want to see volunteers go the distance with you? Then treat them like family by engaging them in relationship.

Relationships form and flourish in a culture of FUN.

Great volunteer teams have a blast serving together. They engage with each other beyond just the "work" of the ministry. They laugh together, play together and have lots of fun together. You see lots of smiles and there's an underlying spirit of joy. Serving is something they look forward to instead of something they endure.

Build a culture of fun by getting together with no agenda except fun. Hang out together. Eat together.

Play games together. Share personal stories. Talk about life together. Consider hosting these meetings away from church property. Go to someone's house, a park, a lake, or some other community place. Be the first to arrive and the last to leave. Don't be behind the grill cooking the hotdogs. Find someone else to do that. Spend your time talking with and getting to know your volunteers.

"Take serving seriously...but not so seriously that you don't engage in fun together!"

Have parties together. Christmas parties. 4th of July fireworks. Labor Day picnics. Memorial Day cookouts. Look for opportunities to get your families together.

Spend time together doing fun things outside of church. Find common interests and hobbies and use it to grow your relationships with your volunteers. Jessie is a volunteer who serves on the safety and security team. He has an amazing testimony. He was born in Liberia where his father was a high-ranking official in the government. When he was just a small boy, there was an uprising in the country and rebels took over. Jessie shared with me how late one night, the rebels came to his house, looking for his father. His mother grabbed he and his brothers and hid in a closet. The rebels came into the house and murdered his father while he listened from the closet. The rebels then began searching the house for other family members to kill. They looked every-where, except the closet he was hiding in. He miraculously escaped with his mother and brothers and came to the United States. His aunt is still there in Liberia and is currently the president of the country at the time of this writing. Jessie and I have something in common. We both love football… specifically our favorite team is the Dallas Cowboys (you either love or hate me now). I wanted to spend some time hanging with Jessie so I invited him to travel with my son and I to see the Cowboys play in Dallas. We had a great time and it made our relationship stronger.

When you meet for training, engage in a fun icebreaker or team building activity. This not only brings the fun factor, but brings the team closer together as well.

Here are ten icebreakers/activities you can use for upcoming meetings.

2 Truths and a Lie

Have everyone secretly write down two truths about themselves and one lie on a small piece of paper. Go around and have people read their three statements. Have everyone try to guess which one is the lie. This activity encourages better communication and helps you get to know each other better.

Egg Drop

Split the group into teams. Teams work together to build an egg holder that can sustain an eight-foot drop. Provide a variety of materials such as paper towels, tape, cardboard, yarn, etc. Give teams 10-15 minutes to build their holder. Have groups take turns dropping their egg and see if it survives the fall. This activity teaches team members to work together and communicate. You can follow up with some debrief questions like:

- How is protecting the egg like protecting our vision?

- What did you learn about teamwork?

- You worked together to keep the egg from cracking when it was dropped. How can we work together to see kids' faith not crack when they grow up?

Marshmallow Spaghetti Tower
Prepare 20 sticks of uncooked spaghetti, 1 roll of masking tape, 1 yard of string and 1 marshmallow for every team. Using these supplies, see which team can build the tallest tower. The challenge? The marshmallow must be at the very top of the spaghetti tower and the whole structure must stand on its own. You can follow up with some debrief questions like:

- How did you work together to build your tower?

- How is this like working together to build our ministry?

- How can we work together to see kids' faith stand strong?

Back-to-Back Drawing
Have everyone pair up. Working in pairs, one person must describe a shape without naming it, while their partner must try to draw the shape they are describing and get as close to the original shape as possible. This activity helps foster better listening and communication between volunteers.

Puzzle Race
Purchase several of the same puzzle. Puzzle should contain 60 pieces or less. Teams race to see who can complete their puzzle the fastest. This activity promotes teamwork and communication. Here are some debrief questions you can ask.

- What did you do to see the big picture come together?

- How is this like what we do in our ministry?

- Why is every piece of the puzzle important?

- How is this like everyone's roles in our ministry?

Turn Over a New Leaf
Have everyone stand on a sheet of plastic. The group must slowly flip the sheet to the other side without anyone stepping off it. This activity helps promote cooperation, trust and communication. Here are some debrief questions you can ask.

- What did it take to turn over the plastic?

- How is this like making needed changes in our ministry?

Finish the Sentence
Gather everyone in a circle. Have someone finish the sentence. Below are some examples. This is a great way for volunteers to get to know each other better and build their relationships. If you'd like to initiate deeper conversations, ask them to explain their answer in more detail.

- I am…
- I have never…
- I love to…
- I would never…
- The best way for me to relax is…
- The funniest thing that ever happened to me was…
- The most important decision I ever made in my life was…
- If you could choose your age forever, what age would you choose and why?

- If you could be in the movie of your choice, what movie would you choose and what character would you play?
- If you could meet any historical figure, who would you choose and why?
- If you were a candy bar, which candy bar would you be? Share why.
- If you were stranded on a desert island, what three items would you want to have with you?
- The most unbelievable thing…
- What favorite color are you and how does being that color make you feel?
- If you could choose an imaginary friend, who would you choose and why?
- If you could sit on a bench in some beautiful woods, who would you like sitting next to you on the bench and why?
- Are you sunrise, daylight, twilight or night? Please share why you picked your time of day?
- The thing that makes me laugh is…
- There is nothing I enjoy more than…
- If I had a time machine, I would go back to visit...
- The best present I ever received was...
- My favorite place to eat is...
- My favorite holiday is...

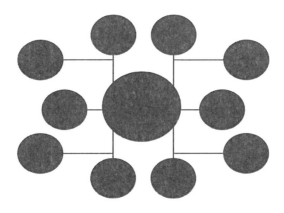

Human Knot

Have everyone stand in a circle facing each other, shoulder to shoulder. Instruct everyone to put their right hand out and grab a random hand of someone across from them. Then, tell them to put their left hand out and grab another random hand from a different person across the circle. Within a set time limit, the group needs to untangle the knot of arms without releasing their hands. If the group is too large, make multiple smaller circles and have the separate groups compete. This activity relies heavily on good communication and teamwork. Here are some debrief questions you can ask:

- How did you work together to get untangled?

- How is this like working together on our team?

Group Juggle

Have everyone stand in an inward facing circle. Ask the group to toss a ball among themselves in a specific order. As the activity develops, more balls are introduced and the pressure to work well as a group increases. Here are some debrief questions you can ask.

- How did it feel when more balls were added?

- How is this like what can happen in our ministry?

- What did it take to keep the balls going?

- What does it take to keep our ministry going?

Some of my dearest friends are people I met through serving. One of them was Howard. He was a big man. When he was a police chief, they called him Howard "Bull" Bennett. He was also a trophy of God's grace. A professing atheist, his his wife had prayed for him for years. He finally came to church and had an encounter with God that changed his life. He was transformed into a new man with a big heart for serving Jesus.

Howard loved creating things on his computer. Retired from the police department, he would spend hours working on his home computer. One way he served was by helping me design children's ministry brochures, handouts and activity pages. I would go to his house each week and sketch out for him what needed to be designed. He would then spend hours working on the projects.

Howard and I not only shared a passion for children's ministry, but for football as well...and we loved the same team... the Dallas Cowboys. He had a plaque hanging above his desk of the 1992 Super Bowl championship team. We would talk about how the season was going when they were playing.

One afternoon, the phone rang. It was Howard's wife, Mary. She was crying and extremely upset. She said Howard had been sitting at his desk and had suddenly passed out and fell back in his chair to the ground. He was unconsious and wasn't responding. I jumped in my car and rushed to the house. The paramedics were already there and were trying to revive him. I held Mary's hand as we prayed for him to be okay. They tried to bring him back....but he was gone. He had suffered a massive heart attack. He had passed away doing what he loved...serving God with his computer.

I spoke at Howard's funeral and shared about the wonderful times we had serving together. After the funeral, Mary handed me Howard's Cowboy's plaque and said, "Howard would want you to have this." I keep the plaque in my office and when I look at it, I think of Howard and remember him. He taught me that God's grace can reach anyone...even an atheist. He taught me to use the gifts God has given you to reach people. He taught me to serve faithfully...all the way...until God calls you home. I miss him. I will see him again. I'm so thankful for all the amazing volunteers I've had the privilege to know and serve with over the years. I'm a better person because of their friendship.

Talk About It...

How well do we engage volunteers through relationship?

How can we see relationships form and flourish by creating a culture of faith?

How can we see relationships form and flourish by creating a culture of family?

How can we see relationships form and flourish by creating a culture of fun?

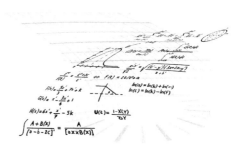

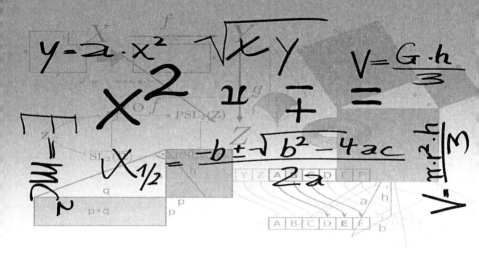

Action Steps

1.

2.

3.

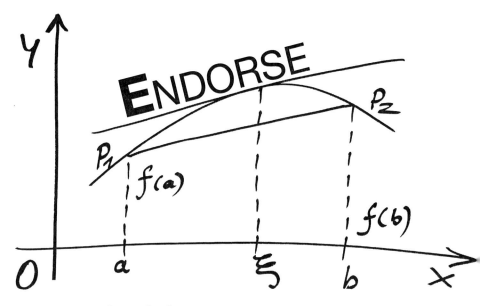

*"Our chief want is someone who will inspire us
to be what we know we could be."*
Ralph Waldo Emerson[1]

Enlist is bringing a volunteer on your team. Equip is setting him or her up for success. Engage is connecting with the person relationally. Which brings us to the next part of the formula. **Endorse. Endorse is putting your stamp of approval on a volunteer.**

Don't assume that your volunteers know they matter. Tell them. Remind them that they matter and what they do matters...a lot. Affirm the gifts God has placed in their life and help them develop those gifts for God's glory. What a privilege we have to build up volunteers by endorsing them.

Be your volunteers' biggest fan. They should know you've got their back and that you're on their side.

Help volunteers see the gifts and abilities God has placed inside them. Sometimes volunteers won't be able to see it because of past rejections, fears, doubts or insecurities. Endorse them by helping them see the potential they have in

Christ. Have faith in them when they don't have faith in themselves. Believe in them even when they can't seem to believe in themselves. God will use your endorsement to instill confidence and courage into their life. I remember when I first met Sherry (name changed) and her family several years ago. They came to our church broken. She had been the children's ministry director at another church and had to leave because the pastor she served under was verbally abusive. When she left, he told her she would never amount to anything for God's kingdom and didn't have what it took to lead a ministry. As she began volunteering with us, we began to speak words of affirmation and endorsement back into her life. She regained her confidence as we shared with her that her former employer was wrong. God had given her many gifts and abilities and she could be a great leader. As we continued to endorse her, she flourished. She now is the director at one of the church's campuses and does an amazing job.

God wants to use you to be the catalyst that helps volunteers discover what is lying dormant inside them. Call out those gifts and abilities and you will stand back in amazement as the person flourishes.

Value volunteers. When you endorse your volunteers, they will feel valued rather than used.

Endorse volunteers by asking for their input and ideas. This shows you respect their opinions and insight.

Endorse volunteers by listening to them. Really listen. This means listening without thinking about what you're going to say next.

Endorse volunteers by communicating with them. It's important to communicate with your volunteers each week through email, text messages, social media and phone calls.

"You can't keep volunteers in the dark during the week and expect them to shine on Sunday."

Endorse volunteers by promptly returning their phone calls and emails. Get back to them in 24 hours or less. This shows they are important to you.

Endorse volunteers by following through on your promises. Make your word your bond. If you're like me, I have to write down my promises if I'm going to remember them. On weekends, I make notes in my phone when I make a promise to a volunteer and then transfer it to my to-do-list on Monday. I remember one weekend, I promised someone I would get a clock for a room. I made a note and on Monday took care of it. I knew the next weekend, the person would be looking for the clock to see if I followed through on my promise. The next weekend, when the person saw the clock was there, without words it communicated, "I value you and care about you enough to follow through on promises I make to you."

Endorse volunteers with your words. There is so much power in the words you speak to your volunteers. It can be life-changing for them. One of the people God used to encourage me was Dr. Ronnie Floyd. When I served on his team, it was the first time I had served in a megachurch and I wondered if I was up to the task. But Dr. Floyd spoke four words to me on several occasions that breathed life, confidence and assurance into my life. He said, "I believe in you." God used those words to encourage me and grow me beyond what I thought was possible on my own. Who can you endorse with your words today? Who can you breathe confidence into today? Who is the person who can be propelled forward today by your endorsement?

Endorse volunteers by showing them kindness and respect. It's not just WHAT you say, but HOW you say it. I remember an incident, when I was stressed out and spoke unkindly to a group of our volunteers. As soon as I said it, I saw their countenance drop and knew I had made a mistake. I apologized and thankfully they forgave me and continued serving. It was a learning experience for me.

Publicly endorse volunteers. A great way to do this is to highlight a volunteer of the month. One way I've done this is by creating a poster each month that features a volunteer of the month. On the poster, we put an endorsement quote about the person.

When you are intentional about endorsing your volunteers, it creates a culture of endorsement and volunteers will also begin endorsing each other. One weekend, we decided to give volunteers Post-It notes and asked them to write down endorsements for their fellow volunteers and then stick the notes on their backs. It spread across the team and was powerful as volunteers endorsed each other.

One of the people they gave an endorsement note to was Rachel. Rachel is a police officer who helps keep our hallways safe on Sundays. Rachel was so blessed that she sent a text thanking us for the endorsement note she received. She even laminated the notes and put them up in her office at the police station. People long for someone to believe in them!

Endorse as God's endorses. In 1 Samuel 16, God tasked Samuel with identifying the next king of Israel. He told him it would be one of the sons of Jesse. When Samuel arrived at Bethlehem, he took one look at the tall and handsome Eliab and thought he must be the one. But God said no...he may appear to be the most likely to succeed...but he's not my choice.

Down the line Samuel went...seven sons...seven likely choices...seven "no's" from God. "Any more sons?" Samuel asked. There was one more... but he was the youngest. Given the lowly job of watching the stinky, dirty sheep...was David...the most unlikely child to be chosen as king.

So unlikely they didn't even bother bringing him to the draft. But God made it clear to Samuel that David was the one.

If a vote were taken, who would be considered the most unlikely volunteer to succeed in your ministry? You know, the volunteer who doesn't have all the natural talent and abilities. That may be the volunteer God has His eye on. That may be the volunteer God has big plans for. That may be the volunteer God wants to use in unbelievable ways!

"God loves to take the most unlikely to succeed and turn them into success stories through His power."

Paul said it so well in 1 Corinthians 1:26-29.

*"Remember, dear brothers and sisters, that few of you were wise in the world's eyes or powerful or wealthy when God called you. Instead, **God chose things the world considers foolish in order to shame those who think they are wise. And He chose things that are powerless to shame those who are powerful. God chose things despised by the world, things counted as nothing at all, and used them to bring to nothing what the world considers important.** As a result, no one can ever boast in the presence of God."[2]*

May God give us His eyes so we can see the great plans He has for the "unlikely" volunteers in our ministry. May we listen to His voice as He guides us to the unlikely volunteers He has chosen to use in unbelievable ways. May we be like Samuel and speak words of endorsement over them.

When you endorse volunteers, it can turn your ministry around. When Doug Conant became the CEO of Campbell's soup in 2001, the company was in decline and had lost half its market value. But Doug turned it around and the team began setting all-time performance records. The secret? He showed them he believed in them. This included Doug writing over 30,000 personal endorsement notes to team members.[3]

When you endorse a volunteer, you are showing him or her that they are a person of significance. We all want to know that our time here on the earth mattered. We all long to leave our footprint and know that our life made a difference. That's why most people tear up when someone is telling them how they've impacted their life. It's a deep emotional need that we long to see fulfilled.

My wife and I are in the process of moving. We have been married for over 27 years, so we had accumulated a house full of "stuff." Stuff like curio cabinets, couches, tables, dressers, night stands, decorations, bookshelves…all of the normal things you find in a house. When we decided to move, we made the decision to sell everything…and I mean everything, except for our clothes, picture albums and a few family heirlooms. We hired an auction company to come and take everything and sell it. I went to the auction the night everything was sold and watched it go away piece by piece. So, as I am typing this, I am sitting in an empty house. All we have left is one old couch, a TV and a mattress we are sleeping on until the house sells. It's been a stark reminder for me of something. In the end, when everything is stripped away, all that really matters…all that is left…is the people you have impacted and the relationships you have with them. That's it. Everything else falls away. Deep down inside, your volunteers know this and they'll invest their lives in impacting others if you'll show them that they matter and that what they do matters beyond the "stuff."

Talk About It…

Do we endorse our volunteers by regularly asking for their input and ideas? How can we improve this?

Do we endorse our volunteers by communicating with them well? How can we improve this?

How do we publicly endorse our volunteers? What are some additional ways we can do this?

Do we have a culture of endorsement among our volunteers? How can we improve this?

How do we show our volunteers they are significant? How can we do improve this?

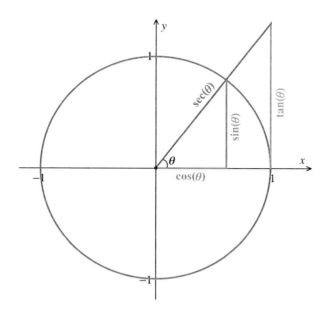

ENDORSE

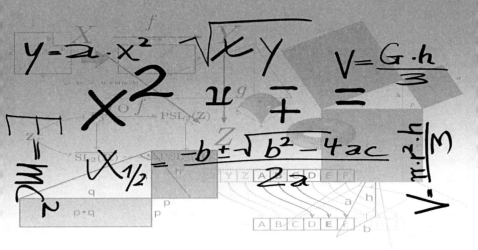

Action Steps

1.

2.

3.

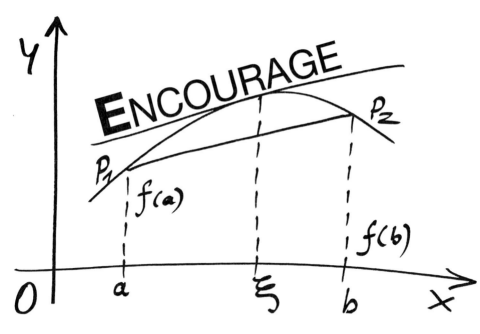

"*Be an encourager: When you encourage others, you boost their self-esteem, enhance their self-confidence, make them work harder, lift their spirits and make them successful in their endeavors. Encouragement goes straight to the heart and is always available. Be an encourager. Always.*"
Roy Bennett[1]

Here's the formula so far for building a great volunteer team.

ENLIST – bring new volunteers on the team.
EQUIP – set volunteers up for success by giving them the knowledge, resources and tools they need.
ENGAGE – build relationships with volunteers.
ENDORSE – validate the gifts and talents God has placed in volunteers.
The next critical part of the formula is **ENCOURAGE**.

Encourage is how you keep volunteers motivated and excited about serving.

Encourage volunteers by
SAYING THANK YOU.

Did you know that 65% of volunteers say they have received no recognition or appreciation in the past 12 months?[2] And then we wonder why they lose heart and get discouraged. Don't be that leader!

Say thank you in person each week. When I am leading a local church volunteer team, every weekend I walk around and say 8 words to the volunteers. They are 8 words that are powerful and help keep your volunteers encouraged. Here they are.

"Thank you for serving and making a difference."

Your volunteers need this from you. Look them in the eye and say these words with sincerity. It will create a culture of encouragement.

Send handwritten thank you notes to your volunteers. In the day of email, text, instant messaging and other forms of digital communication, a hand-written note is golden. Keep a stack of note cards by your desk and each week write a few notes to volunteers. It will mean the world to them. Most of the time they will thank you for the note the next time they see you and many will keep it forever.

Thank them more for who they are more than for what they do. This is a little tweak in the way you say thank you that can make a huge difference. What do we normally say when we are thanking someone? We say, "Thank you for all you _____."

I'm sure you know what the word is – it's "do." The default when we thank someone is to thank them for what they do. And there's nothing wrong with that. But remember, our goal is to show volunteers that we value them not just for what they do for the ministry, but for who they are as a person. If what they do flows from who they are, then that's how we should express our appreciation. Here's an example. Instead of saying, *"Thank for Roger, for teaching the 2nd grade boys' class"* say instead *"Roger, thank for you for your incredible heart for the next generation. Your desire to see the boys grow up to love Jesus inspires us all."*

See the difference? This is the way Paul encouraged believers in the New Testament. Here are a few examples. Check it out.

"We always pray for you, and we give thanks to God, the Father of our Lord Jesus Christ. For we have heard of **your faith** *in Christ Jesus and* **your love** *for all of God's people..."*
Colossians 1:3-4[3]

"I always thank my God when I pray for you, Philemon, because I keep hearing about **your faith** *in the Lord Jesus and* **your love** *for all of God's people."*
Philemon 1:4-5[4]

"Your **strong faith** *in the Lord is like a breath of new life."*
I Thessalonians 3:8[5]

You can see how Paul thanked them for their faith and love. When you thank your volunteers for who they are above what they do, it deepens your encouragement significantly.

Encourage volunteers by
PAYING THEM.

I know what you're thinking. Pay them? I thought they were volunteers! Volunteers don't get paid! Actually, you can pay volunteers. Here's how. **Share with them the stories of lives that have been impacted because of their ministry. That's their pay! That means the world to them!**

Jeremiah was a pre-teen in our ministry. He stepped across the line of faith and accepted Jesus as His Lord and Savior. Shortly after making this decision, it was discovered that he had a brain tumor. He would have to go into the hospital to begin tests. He told his parents he wanted to be baptized before he checked into the hospital. We baptized him on a Saturday night and after the service he went straight to the hospital to begin tests. We continued to pray for his healing. I shared this story with our volunteers. It reminded them that what they do is so important.

Judah was an elementary student that attended our church with his parents. Here's the story behind this. Judah and his family are Jewish. They attended synagogue regularly. His behavior at home and school took a negative turn to the point his parents did not know what to do. They took him to counselors at the synagogue and school, but it didn't help.

Not long after, they were driving by our church and out of desperation decided to come in. They dropped Judah off for our kids' service. When they came to pick him up something had happened to him. He was a different kid. His behavior immediately improved and he was respectful for the first time in a long time. Judah's parents didn't know what Christianity was about, but they did know something good had happened to their son, so they keep bringing him and staying for the adult service while waiting for him. It wasn't long until dad and mom walked forward at the end of a service and stepped across the line of faith themselves. Now the whole family knows Jesus and attends faithfully. We shared this story with our volunteers to remind them that God is using them to reach families.

You have stories like this as well. And these are the kind of stories you want to share with your volunteers. This is their paycheck. This is why they do what they do…they want to be used of God to make an impact. Show them how God has worked through them.

Make sure they know when a family is dedicating their child, when a child steps across the line of faith, when a child follows Jesus in baptism, when a child lives out something they were taught, when an entire family is reached and other examples of fruit from their ministry. Let them know that they had a part in the lives that were changed. Whether they greeted at the door or rocked a baby or taught a class or handed out a craft or led a song…God brought fruit from their ministry.

Pay your volunteers by passing along good reports you receive. When you get a thank you note or email from a family that has been impacted…don't keep it to yourself. Share it with your volunteers.

Encourage volunteers by BRAGGING ON THEM.

Always be looking for opportunities to brag on your volunteers. When the pastor or other church leaders are in your ministry area, introduce one of your volunteers and brag on him or her to the pastor. When you are speaking to a group or gathering and volunteers are present, brag on them for a minute. You can also brag on volunteers on social media. Take pictures of your volunteers in action and then post it on social media. Add comments that highlight their ministry.

"Success as a leader is not found in how many people are bragging on you...it's found in how many people you are bragging on."

Encourage volunteers by
CELEBRATING THEIR MILESTONES.

Celebrate special events in their lives like birthdays, anniversaries, birth of a child, weddings, etc. Celebrate their serving anniversaries and honor them for years of service. Remember to include a personal note that expresses how much they mean to you and the ministry.

Encourage volunteers by
GIVING THEM A SMALL GIFT.

Give your volunteers a small gift several times a year to express your appreciation for them. It doesn't have to be expensive, it's the thought that counts.

Sometimes you should make the gift personal. Here's how you can do this. As mentioned earlier, have each volunteer fill out an information sheet that asks what their favorite food is, what their favorite candy is, what their favorite color is, what their favorite hobby is, etc. Then when you want to give them a personal gift, you can use this list as a reference. Here's an example. You see one of your volunteers loves Three Musketeers candy bars. So, you go and buy him or her that candy bar and attach a personal note to it.

Sometimes you can give everyone on the team the same gift with a creative note. Here are 50 ideas. Yeah... I know a lot of these may seem corny...but volunteers will appreciate even the smallest gift. They simply want to know that you notice them and appreciate what they do.

1. Starburst candy with a note that says, "You're the star of our ministry."

2. Uno candy bar with a note that says, "I hope UNO how much we appreciate you."

3. Lifesaver candy with a note that says, "You're a Lifesaver for the kids."

4. Junior Mints candy with a note that says, "I mint to tell you how thankful I am for you."

5. Reese's Pieces candy with a note that says, "Without you the ministry would fall to pieces."

6. Almond Joy with a note that says, "It's a joy having you on the team."

7. A $5 gift card to Starbucks with a handwritten appreciation note.

8. Homemade cookies with a handwritten note.

9. A bag of microwave popcorn with a note that says, "You are a POPular volunteer."

10. A smores kit with a note that says, "We need smore volunteers like you."

11. Flavored tea bags with a note that says, "You're a Tea-riffic volunteer."

12. A bag of nuts with a note that says, "We're nuts about you."

13. A bottle of A&W root beer with a note that says, "You're an AWesome volunteer."15. Bring them a latte drink and write "Thanks a latte for your heart for the kids" on it.

14. A bag of seeds with a note that says, "Thanks for helping kids' faith grow."

15. Bring them a latte drink and write "Thanks a latte for your heart for the kids" on it.

16. A bag of chocolate chip cookies with a note that says, "Thanks for chipping in to help kids discover Jesus' love."

17. A bag of York Peppermint Patties with a note that says, "Thank you for your commitMINT to the kids."

18. A candle with a note that says, "Thanks for being a light to kids and families."

19. Gift card to a movie with a note that says, "You're the star of our show."

20. Gold Hershey Kisses with a note that says, "You're worth more than gold to us."

21. Gold candy coins with a note that says, "You're CHANGING kids' lives."

22. Fortune cookies with a note that says, "We're so fortunate to have you on our team."

23. Fresh strawberries with a note that says, "We're so glad we picked you to join us!"

24. A small plant with a note that says, "Thanks for planting God's Word in the kids' hearts."

25. A plain coffee mug - write a personal thank you note on it with a sharpie marker.

26. Hand lotion with a note that says, "Thanks for being Jesus' hands and feet."

27. Mountain Dew with a note that says, "Dew you know that we appreciate you!"

28. Certs with a note that says, You CERTainly make a big impact in the kids' lives..

29. Homemade soup with a note that says, "You warm the hearts of kids."

30. Gift card to an ice cream shop with a note that says, "It's a treat having you on the team."

31. Car air freshener with a note that says, "You're a scent-sational volunteer."

32. Twix Bar with a note that says, "Be twix me and you...we couldn't do this without you."

33. Coke with a note that says, "You are so-da bomb as a volunteer."

34. M&M's with a note that says, "Much & Many thanks for your heart for the kids. I appreciate you."

35. Flower with a note that says, "The kids' faith is blooming under your leadership."

36. Extra gum with a note that says, "You are an EXTRAordinary volunteer."

37. Pop rocks with a note that says, "You rock."

38. A Take 5 candy bar with a handwritten note that says, "I wanted to take 5 minutes to write you a note and let you know how much I appreciate..."

39. A bag of Tootsie Rolls with a note that says, "Thank you for the roll you play in helping kids love Jesus."

40. A loaf of fresh baked bread with a note that says, "Thank you for sharing the bread of life with the kids."

41. Box of light-bulbs with a note that says, "Thanks for helping kids have a bright future with Jesus."

42. Nestle Crunch bar with a note that says, "When it's crunch time...we know we can count on you. Thanks."

43. 7-Up with a note that says, "Have a great week...I'll be praying for you all 7 days."

44. Box of donuts with a note that says, "I appreciate you a hole lot."

45. A chap-stick with a note that says, "You're the balm."

46. A roll of Certs with a note that says, "I am CERTainly thankful for you."

47. Swedish Fish with a note that says, "You are of-fish-ially an awesome volunteer."

48. Gummy Bears with a note that says, "The ministry would be unBEARable without you."

49. Blueberry muffins with a note that says, "I am berry thankful for you."

50. 100 Grand Bar with a note that says, "You're priceless to us."

Encourage volunteers by
HAVING AN EVENT TO HONOR THEM.

It's important to show your volunteers how much you appreciate them on a regular basis like we've talked about. The week-by-week pats-on-the-back, thank yous, and encouragement notes are important. Those little expressions of appreciation mean a lot.

But it's also important to "roll out the red carpet" occasionally and go all out to show your volunteers how much they mean to you. This means hosting special events in their honor such as cookouts, dinners and parties.

Encourage volunteers by
BEING THERE FOR THEM.

As a leader of a team, you are a shepherd for the volunteers. This means being there not only to celebrate with them on the mountaintops, but also walking with them through the valleys. Valleys such as sickness, death of a family member, financial hardships, discouragement, kids going astray, injuries and more. Be there for them at the hospital and at the graveside.

There will be many times when you won't know what to say and that's okay. Sometime you don't need to say anything, you simply need to stand by their side and help hold them up. They will remember that you were there for them in their time of need.

Encourage volunteers by
HAVING THE PEOPLE THEY IMPACT THANK THEM.

It means so much to your volunteers to hear from the people they are impacting. **In children's ministry, have special appreciation days where the kids and families bring appreciation notes for the volunteers.** Pause on a regular basis during the children's services and have the kids thank the volunteers for impacting their lives. One of the most impact-ful moments I've seen is kids gathering around their volunteer leader and praying for him or her. It is priceless.

Several years ago, I had a dinner to honor our children's ministry volunteers. I had arranged for parents to secretly bring a dozen or so of the kids to the dinner. After the meal was over, contemplative music started playing and one-by-one the kids walked in and stood in front of the volunteers. They then thanked the volunteers for the impact there were making in their lives. There wasn't a dry eye in the house. Nothing will encourage a volunteer more than hearing from the people he or she is impacting.

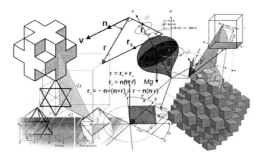

Encourage volunteers by
REMINDING THEM WHY THEY ARE SERVING.

"So let's not get tired of doing what is good. At just the right time we will reap a harvest of blessing if we don't give up."
Galatians 6:9[6]

Even the most committed, faithful volunteers get tired and discouraged at times. If you want to keep them for the long haul, then you have to keep infusing them with energy and passion.

I believe the key is to continually remind them of the impact they are making. In the first chapter, we talked about enlisting people to serve by sharing the why over the what. You encourage people the same way...with the why.

If you don't focus on the why, the what will take over because it is the most obvious. The why is not as immediately visible as the what. Let me give you an example. For someone who volunteers in the nursery, changing diapers (the what) is a lot more tangible than the why (seeing lives changed). For someone who teaches 3rd graders, the what (telling a Bible story) is a lot more tangible than the why (seeing kids grow up to love Jesus). The natural tendency is for the what to overshadow the why.

If you don't keep taking people back to the why, it will be forgotten. Volunteers won't forget the what. They do the what week in and week out. They greet, they hand out crafts, they lead songs, they hold babies, they lead a small group, they pray with kids, they teach preschoolers and all the other whats of ministry. But the why...if you don't take people back to it, can be forgotten over time. People will forget "why" they are doing the "whats" listed above.

If you will keep your volunteers focused on the why, they will remain faithful in the what. When volunteers only see the what, they get burned out. When volunteers only see the what, they lose their passion. When volunteers only see the what, they get discouraged. But when volunteers see the why, they will stay faithful in the what.

You have to be intentional about keeping your volunteers focused on the why. The why doesn't promote itself, you must promote it. The why won't tell its own stories, you must be the storyteller. The why won't celebrate itself, you must celebrate it. When a child steps across the line of faith, let your volunteers know...that's the why. When a young couple's marriage is healed because the volunteers helped watch their baby while they were in a marriage class, let your volunteers know...that's the why. When new families walk in your church doors, let your volunteers know, that's the why. When a child is baptized, let your volunteers know, that's the why. When kids live out their faith, let your volunteers know, that's the why. When a family is reached for Christ, let your volunteers know, that's the why.

The why is what fuels people's passion. I can't say it enough times, volunteers long to be part of something bigger than themselves. Volunteers want to know they are making a difference. Volunteers yearn to be used by God. When you show them how it's happening and they feel the joy and satisfaction that comes from it, they will stay fired up.

"The what...is the car.
The why is the fuel that will keep the car running.
Make sure you keep your volunteers' tanks full!"

Let's take a look at an example with nursery volunteers. They often wonder if they are really making an impact. I mean, you don't see babies memorizing Bible verses or singing worship songs or inviting Christ into their life. So how do you help volunteers who serve in the nursery see they are making an impact? There's a story in Exodus 2 that can be used for this. Let's look at it.

Remember the story of baby Moses? He was born at a time when he shouldn't have survived. Pharaoh was having all Hebrew baby boys killed. But God had His eye on this baby boy named Moses. He had special plans for this kid. Moses' mother hid him for as long as she could, but you can only hide a baby boy with a good set of lungs for so long. So, she made a basket, turned it into a sailboat, and placed him in the river with a prayer and a hope. Check out what happened next.

*"**His sister (Miriam) stood at a distance to see what would happen to him.** Then Pharaoh's daughter went down to the Nile to bathe, and her attendants were walking along the riverbank. She saw the basket among the reeds and sent her female slave to get it. She opened it and saw the baby. He was crying, and she felt sorry for him. 'This is one of the Hebrew babies,' she said. **Then his sister asked Pharaoh's daughter, 'Shall I go and get one of the Hebrew women to nurse the baby for you?'***

*'Yes, go,' she answered. **So, the girl went and got the baby's mother.** Pharaoh's daughter said to her, 'Take this baby and nurse him for me, and I will pay you.'" [7]*

It was no accident that Miriam stuck around to watch over baby Moses from a distance. It was part of God's divine plan. He placed her there to make sure a divine connection would take place between Pharaoh's daughter and Moses' mother. This would allow Moses to be safe in the arms of his mother until it was time for him to go to the palace.

Here's the word of encouragement for nursery volunteers:

- God has a special plan for each child you are watching over.

- You are part of His divine plan for the child's life.

- Sometimes you may feel like you are "watching from the distance" like Miriam was. You may even feel like you are in the "background" because you are not teaching in front of an audience or singing on a stage. But God is working through your life at all times. He does some of His most powerful work in the "background."

- God is using your ministry to make a divine connection in the child's life.

- You never know who you are watching over. The child may be another Moses who changes the world for Christ.

- Keep faithfully watching over the little ones and you will see miraculous things happen.

Here's another example of encouraging volunteers by reminding them of the impact they are making. This example comes from real-life ministry.

Lamont is a big guy. A man's man. He serves on the volunteer security team and helps keep the kids safe while they are at church. This includes locking and unlocking doors, helping walk kids to the bathroom, coordinating the traffic flow when the preschoolers are crossing into the park for chapel, and much more. One weekend, as I was talking with Lamont, God reminded me to tell him something. Here's what I said to him.

*"Lamont, I want you to know that what you do makes a huge impact on families. New families are usually nervous when they walk in here for the very first time. One of the things they are wandering about is if their kids are going to be safe. When they see you, it helps them feel at ease. They can go to the service and listen to the message without being worried about the safety of their child. As a result, many of them come to Christ. And you play a significant part in that. That's **WHY** you're here.*

*You also help kids transition to chapel time where they hear God's Word taught. You make it possible for them to transition safely and you have a part in every child who is impacted by God's Word during chapel time. That's **WHY** you're here.*

*Your smiles and "welcomes" to families make them feel at home. Many of them come back because you helped them feel welcome. As a result, many of them begin a relationship with Jesus. That's **WHY** you do what you do."*

Lamont's eyes lit up. He looked at me, smiled, and said, "thank you." I could tell it meant a lot to him to be reminded of why he is serving.

Here's another example of encouraging volunteers by reminding them of "why" they are serving.

"Thank you for teaching the 2nd graders today." (that's the what)

This is good, but take it to the next level by reminding the volunteer of why they served today.

"Wow...I so appreciate your heart for God and the kids. Because you served today, many of those kids will find Christ as their Savior. And the truths you taught them will impact their lives." (that's the why)

See the difference? Don't just stop with the what - remind them of the why. It will bring encouragement and energy to your volunteers.

Encourage volunteers by
HELPING THEM SEE THE LONG-TERM IMPACT.

Every volunteer has times when they contemplate if it's really worth what they are putting into it. Will they see a return for the investment of their time, energy and resources? Encourage them by helping them see the long-term impact that will come from their serving. They will see some fruit now, but much of it they won't realize until they get to heaven.

I've recently gotten connected with a children's ministry leader who serves in a communist country. He leads an underground network of over 50,000 children's ministry leaders who minister to hundreds of thousands of kids in his country.

I asked him how he came to faith and he shared his story with me. He is a 4th generation believer. In the early 1900's, a missionary from Houston, Texas came to his country and told his great, great grandfather about Jesus. From the seed that missionary planted, has emerged four generations of people serving Jesus in this communist nation.

Wow! Think about the ripple effect that has come from the Gospel pebble that was dropped into the spiritual waters of that country so many years ago. What started as a small ripple has grown into a huge spiritual wave that is impacting hundreds of thousands of people. And the impact continues to spread.

Keep reminding your volunteers, that when they serve, they never know the ripple effect that will come from it. They are creating ripples that will continue for eternity and the full extent of their impact…they won't see until heaven.

Talk About It...

How do we say "thank you" to our volunteers?
How can we improve this?

Do we consistently remind our volunteers of the "why?"
How can we improve this?

On a scale of 1 to 10, how well do we encourage our volunteers? (circle one with 10 being the best)

1   2   3   4   5   6   7   8   9   10

How can we improve this?

How can we help our volunteers see the long-term impact of their service?

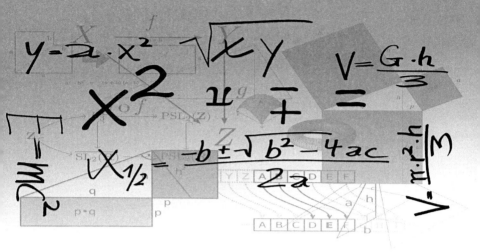

Action Steps

1.

2.

3.

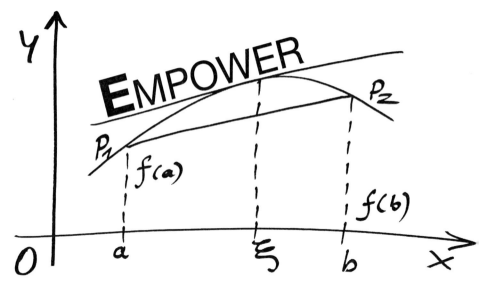

"A leader is best when people barely know he exists,
when his work is done, his aim fulfilled, they will say:
we did it ourselves."
Lao Tzu[1]

The final element of the formula is **EMPOWER.**
Empower is about empowering volunteers and releasing
them to do the work of the ministry. Remember the quote
from earlier?

"It's not what you can do,
it's about what you can empower others to do."

I love what Walt Disney said about the success of his company.

"I don't pose as an authority on anything at all, I follow the
opinions of the ordinary people I meet, and take pride in
the close-knit teamwork with my organization. Whatever we
accomplish belongs to our entire group, a tribute to combined
effort. Everything here at Disneyland and the studio is a
team effort."[2]

You can only take the ministry so far by yourself. If you don't empower volunteers and release them to do ministry, you will become the lid that hinders the ministry from growing and moving forward.

EMPOWERMENT TEST

Want to know how empowered your volunteers are? Here's a simple test. Can you be gone and everything runs smoothly without you? That's a good sign you are empowering others to lead. I love the quote at the beginning of this chapter. It basically says a leader who is empowering others can stand back in the shadows and nothing will miss a beat. And if you're really doing a great job at empowering leaders, it will not only not miss a beat, it will move forward and make progress even without you. We'll talk later about that.

WHAT CAUSES A LEADER TO BE HESITANT ABOUT EMPOWERING VOLUNTEERS?

Are you a control freak in your ministry? If we admit it, we all are to some extent. As we lead our ministries, our desire to bring excellence, passion, and improvement can lead to control issues.

Ownership is vital, but when it becomes unbalanced and leads to unhealthy obsession, it's time for some changes. Though a leader might not say these things out loud, here are some thought patterns that cause leaders to not empower others to help lead the ministry.

"I am a super hero and I can get all this done by myself."
This comes from a desire to prove yourself and show everyone how awesome you are. You don't want to be seen as weak by asking for help. You'll do whatever it takes to prove this – no

matter how many hours you have to work, meals you have to skip or time you have to be away from home. Trust me. The "S" will fall off your shirt. Real super heroes are more empowering than they are powerful.

"Poor me. No one wants to help me. I feel like a martyr."
This comes from a desire to prove your dedication to the ministry. You want everyone to know you are "all in" whether anyone else is or not. If you're not careful, this can lead to feelings of spiritual superiority. Yes, serving is Christ-like, but not just serving alone. Christ empowered others to serve by His side and we are called to do the same. It's not a badge of spirituality to be running around doing everything yourself.

"It will be quicker if I just do it myself."
Yes, maybe this time, but not if you take the long look. When you make time to empower others, you multiply yourself. The time you spend empowering someone will be multiplied many times over.

"I'm afraid I'll be left out of the loop."
It can be hard to give up areas of responsibility...especially the ones you excel at. But you can't get bogged down in the weeds if you're going to lead from a big-picture, visionary perspective.

"They won't do it the right way."
Learn to communicate the level of quality you expect, but don't try to control how the task is done. There is probably more than one way to do the task...and theirs may even be more efficient and effective.

"They can't do it as well as I can."
Even if they can't...sometimes 85% is good enough. The extra 15% that you won't give up may not be as critical as you think it is.

"It's my baby. I don't want to give it up."
You have to give up to go up. Trying to hold onto your "baby" too tightly will hinder the ministry from getting to the next level. It's not about you. Don't let fear keep you from making what could be your greatest contribution to the ministry... letting go and empowering others.

TAKE THESE STEPS TO EMPOWER OTHERS.

"Success in ministry is not about you doing ministry, it's about you empowering others to do ministry."

Identify what only you can do. Resist the urge to lead every project or area of the ministry. Ask yourself these questions.

- Could someone else complete this work to an acceptable level?

- Could someone else do part of this project?

- Could someone else do the initial work so I only have to review and "tweak" it?

- Is this work keeping me from my highest value responsibilities?

Take a pass. Pass on tasks and responsibilities that don't meet the "things only I can do" criteria. This doesn't mean you are being lazy. You're working just as hard, but you're focusing on things that allow you to make the biggest contribution. When you take a pass, it also shows other people that you trust their abilities and contributions.

Follow up. Taking a pass doesn't mean you don't follow up and make sure the task was accomplished. Have accountability and follow-up plans in place. This plays a critical role in making sure the tasks get done. Plans can include regular meetings with key leaders you have given responsibilities. It may mean setting goals and checking progress.

Resist the urge to take back control. Once you start to let go, inevitably there will be a time when something doesn't get done the way that you would prefer. Your gut reaction will be to question why you gave it away. You'll probably say to yourself, "If you want something done right, then you have to do it yourself." But resist the urge. Find out what went wrong. Evaluate and make sure you gave the volunteer the tools, knowledge and resources he or she needed to do the assignment well. Then work with the volunteer to access how to improve it the next time.

LOVE EQUALLY – INVEST SELECTIVELY

As leaders, we are called to love everyone equally. But we are not called to invest in everyone equally. **We must love equally, but invest selectively.** You can only effectively invest in a few people at a time. This means you must be very selective in whom you pick. You must invest your time in people you see potential in. We'll talk more about this at the end of this chapter.

I call this the **Law of the Few**. Choose a few people at a time that you will invest in. The few you invest in will in return invest their time in empowering a few others and the ripple effect will continue to spread. Jesus was a great example of this. He had 12 disciples that He invested in. And inside those 12, He had an inner circle of 3 people that He focused on. The handful that He empowered went out and changed the world.

EMPOWER LEADERS OF LEADERS

In the encourage chapter, we talked about being there for your volunteers. But you must remember, for this to truly be effective and for all volunteers to be cared for, you must empower other volunteers to help with this. You can only effectively lead and shepherd so many people by yourself. Most leaders can care for 6-8 people effectively. Once you reach that limit, the ministry will be capped and will stop growing if you don't raise up other leaders who can care for volunteers as well. In other words, it is vital that you empower volunteers who can lead other volunteers. You can then spend your time empowering the leaders of leaders.

BE A GOOD COACH

As a leader, your role is to be a coach to your volunteers. As their coach, you are to develop them, bring out the best in them, empower them and release them to do ministry. An effective coach meets volunteers where they are and takes them to where they need to be.

A good coach knows the team members. To empower your volunteers, you must understand how they learn best and adjust your methods accordingly. Some of your volunteers learn best by shadowing someone else, some learn best by debriefs, some learn best through goal setting. Others may learn best through analytical thinking and others through quiet practice by themselves. If you want to be a better coach for your volunteers, then ask each of them how they learn best and use their preferred learning style to help them develop.

A good coach provides growth tools. What are some growth tools you can place in their hand? Here are a few examples:

- Take them to a conference with you.

- Send them a link to a podcast.

- Let them know about online conferences and websites.

- Provide them with books to read.

- Take them to visit and learn from other ministries.

- Send them an article that has helped you.

A good coach provides a growth plan. As a coach, you need a plan to develop the volunteers you are investing in. A growth plan is something you and the volunteer can create together. Sit down together and discuss these questions.

- What are some areas you want to improve in as a leader?

- Where would you like to be in one year in those areas?

- What steps can you take to get there?

- What are some specific indicators that will show your progress?

A good coach provides a growth pathway. Out of the growth plan should come a growth pathway. This is a pathway to increased responsibility and influence. We'll talk more about this a little later.

EMPOWER WITH FEEDBACK

"Pity the leader caught between unloving critics
and uncritical lovers."
John Gardener, Leadership Scholar and Presidential Advisor[3]

Feedback is an important part of empowering your volunteers and helping them grow as disciples. Look what the Bible says about this.

"Let us think of ways to motivate one another to
acts of love and good works."
Hebrews 10:24[4]

"Keep putting into practice all you learned and received from
me - everything you heard from me and saw me doing."
Philippians 4:9[5]

There is an art to giving feedback effectively and you can learn it. Here are some tips that will help you become a feedback expert.

Realize that relationship is the starting point for feedback. The old saying is true, isn't it? People don't care how much you know, until they know how much you care. When a volunteer knows you want to see them grow and improve as a leader, they will be receptive to feedback. In fact, if they know you truly have their best interests in mind, they will ask you for it.

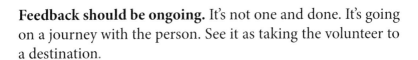

Feedback should be given privately.
Never embarrass someone.

Feedback should be given face-to-face.
Not by phone or email.

Feedback should be ongoing. It's not one and done. It's going on a journey with the person. See it as taking the volunteer to a destination.

Feedback is about focusing on the person more than the tasks assigned. It's about investing in a person.

Feedback should be ongoing. It's not one and done. It's going on a journey with the person. See it as taking the volunteer to a destination.

Give positive feedback when your volunteers do a good job. If you only give negative feedback, volunteers will perceive you as unappreciative and petty.

Avoid giving feedback when it is something the volunteer has no control over.

Avoid giving feedback when a volunteer is highly emotional after a difficult event or experience. Wait a few days so the person will be in a better emotional state to engage with you.

Only give feedback when you can do so in a calm and thorough manner. Feedback should never be given out of anger.

Avoid feedback that is only based on your personal preferences.

When giving a volunteer feedback about an area he or she is struggling in, come with some possible solutions. The purpose of the feedback is to help the volunteer move forward.

Effective feedback asks for permission by using questions like, "Could I offer you a thought?" or "Is this a good time to share a thought with you?"

Effective feedback uses the word "and" instead of "but." When you use the word "but" it causes people to be defensive. Here's an example of this.

> *"You did a good job leading the small group today,* ***but*** *you didn't let the kids ask enough questions."*

Here's an example of doing it the right way by using the word "and:"

"You did a good job leading the small group today ***and*** *I think you can make it even better the next time, if you let the kids ask more questions."*

See the difference? When you use the word "and" it's more collaborative, isn't it?

Effective feedback helps people focus on improving by saying "the next time." Here's an example:

> *"You did a good job leading the small group today and I think you can make it even better* ***the next time*** *if you let the kids ask more questions."*

Effective feedback uses the word "I" instead of "you." When you use the word "you" it sounds like criticism vs. "I" which sounds like advice. Here's an example:

*"**You** need to use more variation in your voice when you're teaching."*

vs.

*"**I** have found that if **I** use variation in my voice, **I** can hold the kids' attention better."*

Millennials and feedback. Studies show that Millennials require more feedback than previous generations. This may be due in part to their upbringing. They have grown up connected from an early age and are used to getting instant feedback from parents, teachers, coaches and friends. They are used to having the immediate ability to ask questions and share opinions. This means they have an ingrained expectation for ongoing communication. But...only 19% of Millennials say they receive feedback. For those who do receive it, only 17% say the feedback they receive is meaningful.[6] A big reason most Millennials don't receive feedback is because even though they want it, they hesitate to ask for it. Only 15% of Millennials routinely ask for feedback.[7] As you lead Millennial volunteers, it's important to take the initiative and ask if they'd like to be given feedback. When you regularly meet with them and give them feedback, their engagement level greatly increases.

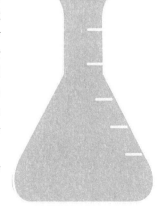

EMPOWER VOLUNTEERS TO GIVE YOU FEEDBACK

Empowering volunteers not only involves giving them feedback, but involves them giving you feedback as well. When you empower volunteers to give you feedback, it shows you value them. It helps them move from being renters to being owners of the ministry. And when volunteers are able to give feedback and be part of the process, you'll get more overall buy in.

See feedback as a gift. First, let's talk about how we view feedback. How do you see it? Do you see feedback as complaining? A necessary evil? A waste of time? Something to be endured? When you begin to see feedback as a gift, you will not only welcome it, you will seek it out. Even the most off-base feedback can contain a small nugget of truth that can make you better as a leader and the ministry better, if you'll listen to it and learn from it.

Build in a rhythm to gather feedback from volunteers. Whether it's once a month, once a quarter or twice a year, create an intentional rhythm in your ministry calendar of gathering feedback.

Gather feedback after events and big programs. Empower volunteers to give feedback after the event. Keep the notes and it can help make the event or program even better the next time. Ask questions like…

- What went well?
- What was missing?
- What needs to be changed?
- What needs to be added?
- What needs to be dropped?
- What will make it better?

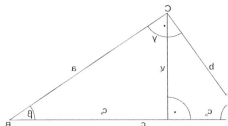

Empower volunteers to give feedback through focus groups. Twice a year gather a group of volunteers for an extended time of feedback. I recommend 8-10 people. Make sure it's a diverse group to get the best feedback. Have some new volunteers, veteran volunteers, student volunteers, senior adult volunteers, etc. Get in a room together and have an in-depth discussion about the ministry. What's working? What's struggling? What feels tired? What needs added? What needs adjusted? What needs changed? How can we make the ministry better? etc.

Empower volunteers to give feedback through online surveys. I have seen great success doing these surveys quarterly. There are many free online options to do these. Limit it to 6-8 questions each time. Here are some topics I've used for the surveys each quarter.

- 1st quarter – Do you feel connected?
- 2nd quarter – Do you feel cared for?
- 3rd quarter – Do you feel challenged?
- 4th quarter – Do you feel celebrated?

Listen to volunteer feedback. Really listen to it. Feedback should primarily be them talking and you asking follow-up and clarifying questions. Take notes on what they are saying.

Thank them for the feedback. Let people know up front how thankful you are for their input and feedback. Also, let them know up front you will sort through it and implement what is doable. Let them know you may not be able to do everything they suggested, but everything will be considered and discussed.

Work through the feedback. Take time to discuss it, evaluate it and process it. Some feedback will be unrealistic, but again, remember there is usually a kernel of truth or help in even the most off-base feedback.

Implement it. Take the ideas that are doable and implement them.

Report back. Report back to those who gave the feedback. Let them know what you are going to be implementing, changing, improving, etc.

PUT VOLUNTEERS IN THE SPOTLIGHT INSTEAD OF YOURSELF

The actions of a leader who empowers others emanates from a heart of servitude. He or she has died to self and is living for others. His or her desire is to shine the spotlight on others instead of self.

Notice the differences between a leader who wants power versus a leader who wants to empower others.

A leader who wants power promotes himself or herself.
A leader who empowers promotes others.

A leader who wants power makes sure he or she shines.
A leader who empowers makes sure others shine.

A leader who wants power is all about "I."
A leader who empowers is all about "You."

A leader who wants power takes credit.
A leader who empowers gives away the credit.

A leader who wants power passes the blame for failure.
A leader who empowers accepts the blame for failure.

A leader who wants power is always on stage.
A leader who empowers puts others on stage.

A leader who wants power develops only himself or herself.
A leader who empowers develops others.

A leader who wants power has to run the show.
A leader who empowers lets others run the show.

A leader who wants power makes sure he or she is the best leader on the team.
A leader who empowers develops people to be even better leaders than he or she is.

A leader who wants power brags on himself or herself.
A leader who empowers brags on others.

A leader who wants power micromanages.
A leader who empowers gets out of the way and lets people lead.

A leader who wants power has all the answers.
A leader who empowers asks a lot of questions.

A leader who wants power does all the talking.
A leader who empowers listens a lot.

A leader who wants power always goes with his or her idea.
A leader who empowers goes with the best idea.

EMPOWERMENT DIMINISHES THE LINE BETWEEN STAFF AND VOLUNTEERS

Walk into a ministry that truly empowers and you'll have a hard time distinguishing between staff and volunteers. Rather than the paid staff running around trying to do everything, you'll find them in the shadows coaching volunteer leaders who are making the ministry happen. **Behind the success of every great ministry is a great team of empowered volunteers who own the ministry and make it happen.** I know many of you who are reading this are volunteer leaders. I'd like to challenge you to continue to grow and increase your volunteer responsibilities. **You are the key to seeing the ministry you serve in move forward.** Perhaps God is calling you to more influence. Perhaps He is calling you to have a greater impact by investing yourself in other volunteers. Perhaps He is calling you to multiply yourself through those you empower. Let your ministry leaders know you are ready to step into the next level of leadership God is calling you to.

EMPOWER VOLUNTEERS TO STAY HEALTHY

As I mentioned earlier, as leaders we are called to shepherd the volunteers that serve with us. This means we help empower them stay spiritually healthy. We want to help them serve from the overflow. Most importantly we want them to grow and prosper spiritually through serving with us.

Make sure they are attending the adult worship service. As they are filled spiritually, they will be able to pour into the lives of others. Make it very clear during the interview and orientation process that all volunteers must attend the adult worship service.

Honor room ratios. It's hard to stay healthy, if you are in a room with 30 preschoolers with one other person. Empower your volunteers by not putting them in this scenario.

Don't ask them to stay over and serve an extra service. A volunteer doesn't show up and you find yourself about to ask the volunteer who is in the room if they will stay over and serve for one more service. Don't do it. It can lead to burnout. Empower them by not putting them in this situation.

Give them time off from serving. You know how you feel when you come back from vacation? You feel rested, refreshed and ready to re-engage. Empower your volunteers by giving them a vacation from serving. Maybe it's a few weeks off during the summer or a Sunday off when it's a 3-day weekend. They'll come back stronger.

Pour into them. We talked about this at length in the equip chapter. It is so relevant to empowering volunteers so they can stay spiritually healthy. Pour into them. Pour into them. Pour into them. Pour into them.

EMPOWER VOLUNTEERS BY INCREASING THEIR INFLUENCE

There is a principle found in Scripture. God honors faithfulness with increased influence. Check out these verses.

"Whoever can be trusted with very little
can also be trusted with much..."
Luke 16:10[8]

"The master said, 'Well done, my good and faithful servant. You have been faithful in handling this small amount, so now I will give you many more responsibilities. Let's celebrate together'!"
Matthew 25:23[9]

As volunteers grow and prove themselves faithful, increase their scope of influence and responsibility. In the most recent children's ministry I led, we had over 70 children's ministry staff members. 65 of them started out as volunteers. As we empowered them and invested in them, we saw them grow into staff leadership roles. When you invest in people and empower them, you will see them flourish as leaders.

We mentioned earlier about creating a leadership pathway. This is where this comes into play. Here's an example. Someone starts out as a helper in a preschool room. Their next step would be leading a preschool room. The next step after that could be overseeing three preschool rooms. Their next step could then be overseeing an entire hallway. Make sure your volunteers know the pathways that are available for them.

"When you empower leaders, you multiply your influence and ensure the ministry will flourish after you're gone."

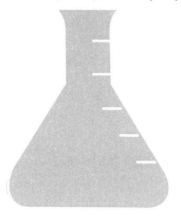

EMPOWER VOLUNTEERS WHEN THEY ARE STRUGGLING

If you will do the things above, it will help volunteers stay healthy and avoid burnout. But no matter how diligent a shepherd you strive to be, there will still be times when you will see a volunteer struggling. And by the way, as a shepherd, we should know our volunteers well enough to recognize when they are struggling. Yes, sometimes a volunteer can put on a mask and fool you, but that should be the exception. Jesus said, *"My sheep hear My voice and I know them."* Make sure you're doing what Jesus modeled for us and know the state of your volunteers.

Here are some signs a volunteer is struggling:

The volunteer starts to show up late for their assigned role. Whereas they used to be on time or even early, they are now consistently late.

The volunteer begins showing up unprepared. They used to care about the little things that add up to an excellent class time, but now they let them slide. You begin to hear "they're just kids, they won't notice."

The volunteer seems distant in conversation. You can sense they are pulling away.

The volunteer is doing the very minimum to get by. They used to go the second mile. Now they slip in and out as quickly as possible.

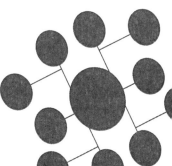

The volunteer begins displaying a negative attitude. You hear from other volunteers that the person is grumbling, complaining and starting to cause dissension.

Strained relationships with other volunteers. Other volunteers come to you about the person becoming abrupt, short-tempered or angry. You know the Snicker's commercial - *"you're not yourself when you're hungry?"* That pretty much sums up how the person begins acting.

You can see the volunteer's enthusiasm is waning. You can tell they are starting to just go through the motions.

The volunteer begins serving less consistently. They start calling in at the last minute to say they will not be able to make it.

The volunteer starts missing training meetings. Whereas they used to be the first one there for training, now they hardly attend.

If you know to look for these early warning signs, you can intervene and help empower the person to re-engage and get back to a healthy place. **Here are some steps to take.**

Ask to meet with the volunteer privately. When you see any of the signs above, meet with the person in private and have a heart-to-heart talk. Again, this must be grounded in relationship.

Find out the root cause behind the symptoms. The signs we listed are simply symptoms of a deeper issue. When you meet with the person, find out what it is. Perhaps they are going through a tough time at work or home or experiencing a spiritual challenge or turmoil in their life.

Offer to come alongside them. How can you support them? How can you help them? How can you walk with them through what they are facing?

Help them navigate their next step. What do they need? Time off? A new role? Counseling? Support from a small group? Financial assistance?

Pray with and for them. There is nothing more empowering than prayer. Take time to pray with the volunteer right then and there. Ask God to meet their needs and encourage their heart. Add the person to your prayer list if they are not already on it. I am reminded of how Jesus told Peter, *"Satan has asked to sift each of you like wheat, but I have pleaded in prayer for you, Simon, that your faith should not fail...." (Luke 22:31-32).*[10] A shepherd prays for his or her volunteers.

WHAT ABOUT A VOLUNTEER WHO IS DISPLAYING TOXIC BEHAVIOR THAT IS AFFECTING THE TEAM?

Sometimes a volunteer will be struggling to the point where his or her behavior becomes toxic and is affecting the team as a whole. In this situation, it is critical that you not react, but act. The unity of the team must be protected. Here are steps to take.

Step One - As mentioned previously, try to find out the root cause of the toxic behavior.

Step Two - Ask if you can give the person feedback. In some cases, the volunteer is oblivious to their toxic behavior. You can't expect a person to change if they don't know they need to. It's important to give them direct and honest feedback so they can understand the problem. Help them see how the behavior is impacting other volunteers and the spirit of the team.

Step Three - Give the volunteer clear steps they can take to turn things around. Don't stop at telling them what the issue is. Point them to the behavior you'd like to see. Help them develop a plan to get there. Give them clearly defined, measurable steps they can take and set a time frame. By doing this, you're giving them an opportunity to have a more positive impact.

Step Four - If the person refuses your help or doesn't show any improvement in the time frame you set for them, explain what the consequences will be if it continues. It may mean being removed from a position of influence. It may mean taking time off from serving until things change. It may mean stepping down from serving completely.

Step Five - Have the courage to follow through with the consequences if there is no change. Your prayer and hope is that God will use this to help the person change. But not everyone will respond. Some will be unwilling to change. If the person is continuing to hurt the morale of the team, then the consequences must be enforced.

Step Six - Document it. Each step of the way, document their offenses, your conversations with them and their responses. Put in writing their behavior, the steps you took to address it, resources and help you offered and the failure of the person to change. It is also good to have someone else with you as a witness when you meet the person.

Remember, you are responsible to people, but not for people. Will some people refuse to grow and change no matter what you do? Yes. Will some people push away from you even as you offer to help them? Yes. But don't let it discourage you. You are a shepherd. Be the best shepherd you can be for the volunteers God has placed in your care and you will see many of them serve with you for the long haul.

A CLASSIC EXAMPLE OF VOLUNTEER EMPOWERMENT FROM SCRIPTURE

Recently, I was reading God's Word and came across a great Biblical example of empowering volunteers. It contains so much wisdom about empowering others. Check it out with me. It is found in 1 Kings 19 & continues in 2 Kings 2.

"So Elijah went from there and found Elisha son of Shaphat. He was plowing with twelve yoke of oxen, and he himself was driving the twelfth pair. Elijah went up to him and threw his cloak around him. Elisha then left his oxen and ran after Elijah. 'Let me kiss my father and mother goodbye,' he said, 'and then I will come with you.' 'Go back,' Elijah replied. 'What have I done to you?'

So Elisha left him and went back. He took his yoke of oxen and slaughtered them. He burned the plowing equipment to cook the meat and gave it to the people, and they ate. Then he set out to follow Elijah and became his servant. When they had crossed, Elijah said to Elisha, 'Tell me, what can I do for you before I am taken from you?'

'Let me inherit a double portion of your spirit,' Elisha replied. 'You have asked a difficult thing,' Elijah said, 'yet if you see me when I am taken from you, it will be yours - otherwise, it will not.'

As they were walking along and talking together, suddenly a chariot of fire and horses of fire appeared and separated the two of them, and Elijah went up to heaven in a whirlwind. Elisha saw this and cried out, 'My father! My father! The chariots and horsemen of Israel.' And Elisha saw him no more.

Then he took hold of his garment and tore it in two. Elisha then picked up Elijah's cloak that had fallen from him and went back and stood on the bank of the Jordan. He took the cloak that had fallen from Elijah and struck the water with it.

'Where now is the Lord, the God of Elijah?' he asked. When he struck the water, it divided to the right and to the left, and he crossed over. The company of the prophets from Jericho, who were watching, said, "the spirit of Elijah is resting on Elisha".[11]

Elijah was a mighty prophet of God. He was a bold prophet. He was an anointed prophet. He stood alone against 850 of Baal's false prophets and saw God reign down fire from heaven to bring a great victory. As Elijah began to prepare for his transition, he began to look for someone he could mentor and raise up to be the next prophet of God. Someone that he could hand down his cloak to. His cloak represented the ministry and anointing God had placed upon Him.

Elijah successfully handed down his anointing and ministry to Elisha. It culminated with his cloak falling off his back and into Elisha's grasp.

Just like Elijah, you and I are called to hand down to others the leadership and ministry God has entrusted us with. From Elijah's example, here are the keys to a successful leadership hand-me-down.

Leadership Hand-Me-Downs involve THINKING

Human nature skews us toward building our own kingdom. We want the spotlight...the glory...the praise and accolades. What if the person we develop outshines us? What if they take the ministry farther than we could?

But a hand-me-down means you think differently. You die to yourself and esteem others better than yourself. You begin to live Philippians 2:3 which says,

"Don't be selfish; don't try to impress others. Be humble, thinking of others as better than yourselves."[12]

Elijah reached the point where it wasn't about him. It was about the mission. He realized that what he was part of was bigger than the part he played. A successful hand-me-down starts first with you. Are you willing to adjust your thinking and say, "It's not about me?" Are you willing to help others rise above you? Are you willing to let others go farther than you have gone?

Leadership Hand-Me-Downs involve THROWING

If you look back at the passage, you'll notice that Elijah went, found Elisha and threw his cloak on him. Developing leaders requires intentionality. You must go to the right person and make the ask.

The big question...how do you know who the right person is? The answers can be found in the passage. Here's what to look for when you're searching for someone to invest in.

Look for someone who wants to fulfill God's will for their life. The person should have a sense of calling. Notice how Elisha engaged and began following Elijah. He was ready to find the destiny God had for him.

Look for someone who is all in. Elisha was willing to leave his family, financial security and home to follow God's call. Look for someone who is already committed. Look for someone who already goes the second mile. Look for someone who is already serving faithfully.

Look for someone who is willing to pay the price. As referenced above, Elisha was willing to let go of his financial livelihood to fulfill God's destiny for his life. He slaughtered his oxen and burned his plowing equipment. He made it clear there was no turning back.

Look for someone who is willing to serve first. Notice what it says about Elisha at the end of chapter 19. It says, *"He set out to follow Elijah and serve him."* Great leaders are great followers first. They are more concerned about serving others than they are about getting a title.

Look for someone who has a teachable spirit. If the person is not teachable, they will not be usable.

Look for someone who has what can't be taught. These are things like character, integrity, passion and motivation. People either have them or they don't. Notice how Elisha was self-motivated. He asked for a double portion of the anointing that was on Elijah's life.

Look for the person who emerges from the crowd. There were many young prophets at the time. But it was Elisha that emerged from the crowd as the obvious choice. As I shared earlier, raising up a leader is not the time for charity cases. Love everyone equally, but be very selective in whom you invest in.

Leadership Hand-Me-Downs involve TRAINING

Elijah took Elisha with him on the journey and trained him along the way. It takes work to develop a leader. It takes lots of teaching, showing, providing feedback, mentoring, talking, praying and investing. Once again, is it faster to do ministry by yourself? Yes. But the ministry will go farther if you bring someone with you.

Leadership Hand-Me-Downs involve
TIMING

The hand-me-down wasn't done immediately. Timing is important in such matters. God's timing came one day as they stood together by the Jordan River. As Elijah was caught up into the heavens, his cloak was left for Elisha. The transfer was made. The hand-me-down was complete.

Timing is important in your hand-me-down as well. A premature hand-me-down can result in the successor not being prepared or ready to lead. An overdue hand-me-down can result in stagnation and discouragement. The right timing comes from God's wisdom and guidance being infused into the process.

Leadership Hand-Me-Downs involve
THRIVING

When you develop leaders effectively, the ministry will thrive. Elijah did 14 miracles. Guess how many Elisha did? 28. Exactly double...right in line with the double portion he had asked for. I can't help but think that Elijah looked down from heaven and rejoiced.

Our prayer should be that the leaders we develop will make the ministry twice as good as we could have alone. That they will reach twice as many people. That they will see twice as many miracles. That they will see twice as many blessings. That they will be twice as good as leaders as we were. A truly effective hand-me-down results in the ministry thriving instead of just surviving!

Who will you throw your cloak upon? Who will you raise up to lead with you now and later after you are gone? Who is your Elisha?

Start **THROWING** your cloak on the person God wants you to develop. Pour yourself into **TRAINING** that person. In God's **TIMING**, advance them. Watch the ministry begin **THRIVING**.

Talk About It...

Do we pass the empowerment test? Can the staff or key volunteer leader be gone and things still not miss a beat? Why or why not?

Who are the key volunteers that we need to invest in?

How well do we coach our volunteers? Do we provide them with a growth plan and pathway? How can we improve this?

Are we giving our volunteers feedback to help them grow? How can we improve this?

Are we gathering feedback from our volunteers? How can we improve this?

How are we empowering our volunteers to stay spiritually healthy? How can we improve this?

How well do we know our volunteers? Have we established a relationship that is deep enough to speak into their lives? How can we strengthen the relationship we have with them?

Who has proven themselves faithful and needs to be approached about taking on more responsibility and influence?

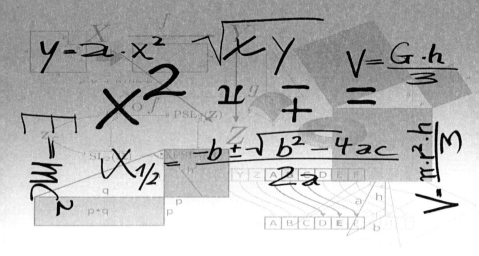

Action Steps

1.

2.

3.

ENDNOTES

ENLIST

1. Walt Disney, http://www.disneyanimation.com/studio/studiolife.
2. Matthew 28:19, NLT.
3. Ephesians 4:11-16, NLT.
4. James 2:26, NLT.
5. Mark 10:45, NLT.
6. Dr. Martin Luther King, http://www.thekingcenter.org/get-involved.
7. Ephesians 2:10, NLT.
8. http://www.factsforlifeglobal.org/03/.
9. Lisa Rowland quoting George Barna, http://bwchurch.org/are-you-a-distracted-parent/.
10. Matthew 9:9, NLT.
11. http://www.wral.com/news/local/story/3296544/.
12. http://blogcritics.org/teen-choice-awards-recognizes-teens-who/.
13. http://www.prnewswire.com/news-releases/teenchoice-awards-2008-recognizes-northwest-teen-dallas-jessup-57556447.html.
14. http://myhero.com/hero.asp?hero=Pat_Pedraja_Brick08.
15. http://www.pewresearch.org/fact-tank/2016/04/25/millennials-overtake-baby-boomers/.
16. Shana Lebowitz, http://www.businessinsider.com/deloitte-chairman-how-to-retain-millennial-employees-2016-2.
17. https://en.wikipedia.org/wiki/Silent_Generation.
18. https://en.wikipedia.org/wiki/Silent_Generation.
19. Susan Pettine quoting David Eisner, report introduction, The Relationship of Leadership Styles and Recognition of Retiring Boomers as Potential Volunteers: A Study of Nonprofit Administrators, 11/2006.

20. Robert Grimm, http://nbcb.blogspot.com/2007/03/non profits-should-target-boomers.html.
21. https://www.nationalservice.gov/sites/default/files/documents/boomer_vol_0.pdf.
22. https://www.nationalservice.gov/pdf/07_0307_boomer_report.pdf.
23. John 1:40-42, NLT.
24. Matthew 9:35-38, NLT.

EQUIP

1. Ephesians 4:12, NLT.
2. Jeff James, Vice President & General Manager of Disney Institute,https://disneyinstitute.com/blog/2014/ 02/optional-or-operational-the-case-for-great-training-/238/.
3. Joan C. Williams and Heather Boushey, https:/www.americanprogress.org/issues/economy/reports/2010/01/25/7194/the-three-faces-of-work-family-conflict/.
4. Rafat Ali, https://skift.com/2015/01/05/travel-habits-of-americans-41-percent-didnt-take-any-vacation-days-in-2014/.
5. http://www.projecttimeoff.com/research/work-martyrs-children.
6. Craig Fehrman, archive.boston.com/bostonglobe/ideas/articles/2011/01/02/the_incredible_shrinking_sound_bite/?page=1.
7. Illysa Izenberg, http://www.facultyfocus.com/articles/in-structional-design/the-eight-minute-lecture-keeps-students-engaged/.

ENDORSE

1. Ralph Waldo Emerson, https://www.brainyquote.com/quotes/quotes/r/ralphwaldo130588.html.
2. I Corinthians 1:26-29, NLT.
3. https://www.fastcompany.com/3035830/hit-the-ground-running/how-campbells-soups-former-ceo-turned-the-company-around.

ENDNOTES

ENCOURAGE

1. Roy Bennett, http://www.goodreads.com/quotes/tag/encouragement.
2. http://www.relevantchildrensministry.com/2016/09/3-secrets-to-showing-volunteers-youre.html.
3. Colossians 1:3-4, NLT.
4. Philemon 1:4-5, NLT.
5. I Thessalonians 3:8, CEV.
6. Galatians 6:9, NLT.
7. Exodus 2:4-9, NIV.

EMPOWER

1. Lao, Tzu,https://www.goodreads.com/authorquotes/2622245.Lao_Tzu.
2. Dave Smith quoting Walt Disney, The Quotable Walt Disney, NY, NY, Disney Editions, 2001, p. 98.
3. John Gardner, https://wisdomquotes.com/quote/john-gardner.html.
4. Hebrews 10:24, NLT.
5. Philippians 4:9, NLT.
6. Amy Adkins and Brandon Rigoni, http://www.gallup.com/businessjournal/192038/managers-millennials-feedback-won-ask.aspx.
7. Amy Adkins and Brandon Rigoni, http://www.gallup.com/businessjournal/192038/managers-millennials-feedback-won-ask.aspx.
8. Luke 16:10, NIV.
9. Matthew 25:23, NLT.
10. Luke 21:31-32, NLT.
10. 1 Kings 19:19-21 & 2 Kings 2:9-15, NIV.
11. Philippians 2:3, NLT.